Devotions for Personal and Group Renewal

Devotions for Personal and Group Renewal

Wallace Fridy

ABINGDON PRESS
Nashville and New York

DEVOTIONS FOR PERSONAL AND GROUP RENEWAL

Copyright © 1969 by Abingdon Press

All rights in this book are reserved.
No part of the book may be reproduced in any manner whatsoever without written permission of the publishers except brief quotations embodied in critical articles or reviews. For information address Abingdon Press, Nashville, Tennessee.

Standard Book Number: 687-10647-8

Library of Congress Catalog Card Number: 78-86162

Scripture quotations unless otherwise noted are from the Revised Standard Version of the Bible, copyrighted 1946 and 1952 by the Division of Christian Education, National Council of Churches, and are used by permission.

Scripture quotations noted Moffatt are from *The Bible: A New Translation,* by James Moffatt; copyright 1935 by Harper & Row.

Scripture quotations noted NEB are from the New English Bible, New Testament. © the Delegates of the Oxford University Press and the Syndics of the Cambridge University Press 1961. Reprinted by permission.

SET UP, PRINTED, AND BOUND BY THE
PARTHENON PRESS, AT NASHVILLE,
TENNESSEE, UNITED STATES OF AMERICA

To
George Stewart
Minister-Scholar-Counselor
My Friend

Preface

Every generation faces the task of finding the meaning of faith for its own age. The same is true today. The Gospel does not change, but its implications and applications do.

Paul says in II Cor. 4:7, "We are no better than pots of earthenware to contain this treasure" (NEB). The vessels are forever outmoded, are never the right shape. We must continually be working to remold our thought to make it more suitable to carry the treasure of the Gospel to our culture.

The changing world and our altering culture force us to see our faith in the light of the needs of the age. This involves not only our mission to our times but also the language of our faith. Theology is not static but is always trying to have a word for the time in which it lives. Consequently, there is the necessity of translating the truth revealed in the first century to what it means in the twentieth century. We are to retell the story in our terms for today.

Our job is to penetrate the mind of the first century and to know that something wonderful happened in Jesus of Nazareth—a Power came into life in him that man had never seen before. We must experience this power for ourselves and tell it in the language of our day. This same power that moved so mightily in the world of the first century is at work in our world. What would he have me do?

John Elbridge Hines in his inaugural sermon as presiding bishop of the Protestant Episcopal Church in the United States, cited this aphorism from the late Dag Hammarskjöld: "In our era, the road to holiness necessarily passes through the world of action." Bishop Hines said that the time has passed when Christians can retreat within their ecclesiastical fortress to recite prayers and polish brass. "The church," he emphasized, "is caught up today in the throes of a worldwide convulsion, the basic ferment of which is the thrust for freedom and dignity and hope on the part of the little people of the world. The church as an agent of God's reconciling love cannot survive this revolution as an observer."

In these stirring words the presiding bishop speaks of the church's task out in the world where suffering is, where wrongs are to be righted, where freedom is threatened and denied, where sin abounds. He speaks of the church in mission.

This is the great thrust of the church today: "The road to holiness necessarily passes through the world of action."

These messages are sent out with the hope and prayer that those who read them in private or who are led by them in group worship may find an inward and outward journey which will result in new life in Christ.

WALLACE FRIDY

Contents

News That Can Overcome Your Fear 11
A Power That Can Make Us Whole 16
God's People on Mission 20
God Is Already There 26
A Committed Christian 29
The Dark Night of the Soul 34
Refuse to Pity Yourself 39
Maintaining a Sense of Wonder 42
Being Renewed Every Day 48
And We Are Whole Again 51
The Story of a Prayer 56
We Need a Stalwart Faith 60
Guidelines for Church Renewal 65
The Grace of God 70
Becoming a New Creature 75
Get Up and Walk 81
Days Aren't Long Enough 87
Servants of a Sacred Trust 90
Who Touched Me? 95

DEVOTIONS FOR PERSONAL AND GROUP RENEWAL

For Special Days and Seasons

More Than We Are (World Day of Prayer) 100
A New Commandment (Lent) 107
Taking It upon Himself (Palm Sunday) 111
He Bore the Cross of Christ (Good Friday) 116
The Future Belongs to Love (Easter) 122
The Jobs We Do (Labor Day) 126
Living in Expectation (Advent) 131
Our Bible Comes Alive (Universal Bible Sunday 136
Christmas Is a Time for Giving (Christmas) 141

News That Can Overcome Your Fear

In a recent popular magazine this question was asked: "What are you afraid of?" The magazine article portrays for us photographic studies of people who fear sex, insecurity, illness, death, loneliness, and old age. Then it gives advice about how to overcome each fear. Prefacing its study, it says that fear is common to all people. Some fear is born in us, but most fears begin in early childhood—and all of them can influence our lives for good or evil. Chesterton once said, "If I had only one sermon to preach, it would be against fear." He said this because he knew that fear is one of the most common and crippling of man's enemies.

Joseph Fort Newton, who for eleven years received thousands of letters from readers who read his daily syndicated column "Everyday Religion," reflects upon "what are the things that hold us back from the larger life we want to live? What is it that inhibits us, cripples us, making us victims of morbid fatigue that spoils our joy and defeats our dreams?" One answer burned itself into his heart: Public Enemy Number 1 in human life is neither sin nor sorrow, bad as these can be, but fear. No wonder, he said, that Montaigne wrote, "The thing in the world I am most afraid of is fear."

Yet, having said this, fear is not always a villain.

On the contrary, it may be a benevolent force making us aware of physical dangers. It can be a red-light signal, a "stop, look, listen" sign of impending doom ahead. Fear keeps us from being hit by a train. It discourages us from being content to live in unsanitary conditions, from disobeying the doctor's orders. In a sense, we are blessed by the capacity to know fear. Like opium and alcohol, it does have its worthwhile uses. All inventions are in a measure by-products of fears and worries. Fear has often been the stimulus to growth, and the goad to invention.

But there is a difference between desirable and undesirable fear. A little is necessary, but excessive amounts distort our whole future. So our business, in one sense, is not to get rid of fear but to harness it.

How, then, are we to handle our fears? What is the news that can overcome fear?

It is the good news that you are loved. It is the communication to a person that love abounds. In I John 4:18 we have these words, "There is no fear in love, but perfect love casts out fear." Coupled with this verse is another found in Isaiah:

> For I, the Lord your God,
>   hold your right hand;
> it is I who say to you, "Fear not,
>   I will help you." (41:13)

This is the great need of our time—love which casts out fear. The good news of the gospel is just this: you are loved by God, and this love is communicated by persons. This is what is meant by the incarnation

—God was in Christ, loving the world and all who are in it.

The church should be made up of people who know they are loved by God and who communicate that love to others. This is news that can overcome fear. Thus, in the church we should find this love in action and feel secure in it. Let us make our church such a loving fellowship that all who come into our midst may know that they matter, that they are important, and that they need not be afraid. It is this kind of wine and bread which should be offered to all who come.

When men find within the church fellowship such love, you will not be able to keep them out, for herein is love that can overcome fear—man's greatest enemy.

It is this good news of love which must be communicated to persons in all stages of life. What does it say to little children to make them know this is the Father's world and that it is a good world? What does it say to youth trying to find their way in life? What does it say to those in midstream, and to those facing sunset years?

All appointments in the church should convey warmth and love. Austerity and coolness should be eliminated. There should be joyousness and happiness conveyed. To be sure, the majesty and mystery of God should be felt in our places of worship. Beauty should help to reveal his nature, but through it all, love must abound.

What is involved in communicating to a person that he is loved?

In the first place, it is to accept him for what he is as

a person and child of God. Acceptance is the first word of love. "I accept you as you are."

Acceptance is good news to anyone. It is to feel wanted and to have a place. The degree to which we are accepted or feel accepted is communicated by another person. It has a language all its own. It conveys a message without words. We can give love only to the degree we have received it. The gospel takes place at the point of acceptance. Herein is the good news.

Love does not have the element of force. In a real sense, love is willing to let another go—free to go and be himself. It gives people the right to be wrong.

In the second place, understanding is involved in communicating this love. To really understand is to try and see in others that which made them as they are. It is to try and understand what has produced this reality. It is to acknowledge that what a person does at any given moment seems to him at that time to be the satisfying or reasonable thing to do.

Understanding, next to acceptance, is basic in communicating love. It is a magic word. To say "I understand" conveys a warmth all its own.

A third aspect of communicating love is *the willingness to walk with another so that this person can become the best possible person.* That person becomes the object of genuine concern.

What a wonderful thing happens to a person who knows that there are those who will walk with him so that he might be his best!

The Christian fellowship should be that sort of association, helping those within it to be their best, to become the kind of persons God intended them to be.

Think what this means in upholding and supporting one another. Some time ago during an hour of great bereavement one of our members said to me, "The love about which you have been talking is real here. It has supported us during these days of great anguish and sorrow. It is real, and it is here."

But this supportive role should be manifest not only during hours of sorrow, but through all experiences. We should help our children and youth grow up that they might be their best. All activities of the church should be directed toward this one purpose.

When a person finds himself in a situation where love is communicated through acceptance, understanding, and support to help him be his best, then he is a recipient of the gospel. Herein is good news which can drive out fear.

AIDS TO WORSHIP

Hymns: "O God, Our Help in Ages Past"
"Lord, for Tomorrow and Its Need"
Scripture: I John 4:18-21; Isa. 41:13

A Prayer

O most loving Father, who willest us to give thanks for all things, to dread nothing but the loss of thee, and to cast all our care on thee who carest for us: Preserve us from faithless fears and worldly anxieties, and grant that no clouds of this mortal life may hide from us the light of that love which is immortal, and which thou hast manifested to us in thy Son Jesus Christ our Lord. *Amen.*[1]

---

[1] *The Book of Common Prayer.*

A Power That Can Make Us Whole

To be human is to be aware of the self as an insecure being separated from a power that would make man whole. This idea was expressed by the Rev. Jack Spong in a teaching mission. This insecurity takes all sorts of forms as people try to affirm their being. Some escape through mental and physical illness from the distress areas of life. Some find in alcoholism an escape where they can live in a make-believe land, where little people can become big people. Others escape through dependence upon others. Every human being centers attention on himself—the self he is—and seeks to use people to build himself up.

To be a secure being, to be a whole person, man needs a complete affirmation of self that comes only through perfect love, and no man has this. We need the grace to *love* the self we are, the grace to *be* the self we are, and the grace to *accept* the self we are. God alone represents perfect love, and man has found the source of power and courage in Jesus Christ.

Simon Peter is an example of one who was representative of human weakness. That weakness was shown all through his life. Simon Peter was trying to prove that he was a big man by being a dominating personality. But a dominating personality is always an insecure person. Yet Jesus selected Peter—this weak person—to be a disciple. And Peter in his despair found his strength in Jesus Christ, who picked him up a broken man and made him whole again. Peter discovered the power in Jesus of Nazareth and knew that there was something about him that was of God.

Jesus lived without fear and without defense. He was free of self-concern; he was what he was; he was not "becoming." Jesus of Nazareth was not grasping for selfhood or an other-directed life. Even when he was dying, he was not grasping after life. He was giving it away; and before one can give self away, one has to possess a self. Jesus had a self to give. The only person in history to bring the perfect love of God into human experience was Jesus Christ.

Mr. Spong listed four ways in which Jesus sought to bring the love of God into the lives of people. *First,* he tried through teaching, through words and parables, but people did not really hear him. They tried to use him. And so Jesus failed here in terms of his purpose. *Second,* he tried through demonstrating God's love in healing. He healed the sick so that the love of God might be seen, but people did not see it. They saw Jesus simply as a wonder-worker, and the healing ministry of Jesus failed insofar as his purpose was concerned. *Third,* Jesus tried by concentrating upon the twelve and failed here too: one betrayed him; one denied him; and ten forsook him and fled. They even argued about status symbols. *Fourth,* Jesus tried the only way left open to him—personal example, which meant traveling the path of death. He laid down his life. He allowed men to do the worst they could do to him. This was his last chance, and he deliberately set in motion those forces which led to his death. Jesus realized that he must depend upon men to see the meaning of the love of God as it was revealed on the cross. Men did look upon that cross, and they found that no matter what they were, its power could bring wholeness to them.

After the cross, Peter never again was a frightened man. What he discovered and saw there made him whole.

Thus, to be a Christian is to be what you are in freedom, to be made whole by the love of God, to accept his love. It is to look at your own weakness and to know that you will not be destroyed by it, to see your talents and to use them not as a means to build up your own ego, but as God-given gifts. A Christian is one who lives not just the good life, but the loving life. His is not an imperialistic life, for he allows every man freedom to fulfill his own destiny. The Christian is someone so undergirded by love that he can give love away. He has experienced the love of God and the forgiveness of God in such a way that he is able to forgive other men. The Christian is free to be what he is without being afraid.

This undergirding love of God is found in Jesus of Nazareth and speaks to every human being. Indeed, God was in Christ reconciling—making whole—the world unto himself. This is the loving work of God and enables us to be what we are and to overcome the sin of our lives.

AIDS TO WORSHIP

Hymns: "O Worship the King"
"Love Divine, All Loves Excelling"
Scripture: John 15:1-11

A Prayer

O God, renew our spirits by thy Holy Spirit, and draw our hearts this day unto thyself, that our work may not be a burden, but a delight; and give us such a mighty love to thee as may sweeten all our obedience. Let us not serve with the spirit of bondage as slaves, but with cheerfulness and gladness, as children, delighting ourselves in thee and rejoicing in thy wishes for the sake of Jesus Christ. *Amen.*[1]

---

[1] Benjamin Jenks.

God's People on Mission

In the second chaper of First Peter, verses nine and ten, we have these words: "But you are a chosen race, a royal priesthood, a holy nation, God's own people, that you may declare the wonderful deeds of him who called you out of darkness into his marvelous light. Once you were no people but now you are God's people; once you had not received mercy but now you have received mercy."

This tells us who we are, and who we are supposed to be, God's people, called out of darkness into his marvelous light. I wish that could be said of all whose names are inscribed upon the rolls of the Christian church today.

This is it; we have been called by God, through Jesus Christ, to be built into a spiritual house, to be a holy priesthood. We are God's people on mission. That is, we are called to serve, to be used of him in the world, to be each of us, a priest to every other person. The church does not exist for itself, but for God, as an instrument of redemption for mankind.

To be an instrument of redemption, the church must be made up of redeemed people, committed and dedicated to his service in the world. All that we do should be directed toward our mission in the world. The only real justification for all our buildings and comforts in the institution of the church is that such may be a means of building us up in the faith that we might go on mission for Christ; that we might be better priests to our neighbors; that we might all be ministers to everyone we meet.

The building and the parking lot, the air conditioning and the heat, the fellowship hall and the organ —all are to be aids in preparing us to serve Christ better out in the world. Here is our headquarters. Here is our base. Here is our assembly ground. Out yonder is our field of operation. Out yonder is our church at work in the persons of those who have come to be strengthened in the faith. The institution is not an end within itself, but is merely a necessary means through which we can, we hope, better serve God.

Church work does not consist merely of housekeeping duties—the Martha-kind of activity in committees and meetings—but church work goes on in school board meetings, in city hall, at the grocery store, at the theater, at the school, in the markets of trade, in the home, in the factory, in the office. For here is where we witness to our faith. Here is where our mission operates. Here is where we live so that others will know whose people we are—God's people.

To be God's people on mission implies that we will seek to know God, not just know who he is. To know God we must spend some time with him, we must seek to know his word and his way for life, for life today.

We are God's people on mission not only when we are alone with him in prayer and in the study of his Word, but also when we are in company with his people, especially a small group of his people in whose presence we feel accepted and in whose midst we seek to know what God would have us do.

To be God's people on mission is to seek to be open to the leadership of the Holy Spirit and to be willing to follow to the end what God would have us do at any given moment. It means that we will forever be on the growing edge of new discoveries, for God is alive and active in his world, and we are caught up in his activity if we are his people on mission. Structures will of necessity change with the changing needs of each new age. Institutional forms will alter to meet the demands of the hour in which we live.

All this will bring to God's people the most exciting adventure in life—being on the frontier with him in the building of a better world and being part of a redemptive society.

To be on mission for God involves total commitment to him and his way as we have discovered it in Jesus Christ—commitment of time, strength, talent, money, life. It is to "lay it on the line" for Christ's sake, to be spent and used by him on his mission of the redemption of mankind.

To be on mission for him, God's people rightly expect power and strength from the source and the ground of our being—God.

This commitment requires disciplines whose practice and demands produce faith. What are some of these disciplines which we must keep if we are to be God's people on mission?

For one thing, there must be regularity of prayer and Bible study. Daily we must turn to the Scriptures

GOD'S PEOPLE ON MISSION

for direction and for revelation of God through Christ, who reaches out to meet us through these pages. If we are to be his people on mission in this world, we should ask him what it is he wants us to do and to be. The fact is, without this regularity of study and communication we cannot, with faithfulness, be God's people on mission in his world.

Second, there must be regularity of proportionate giving to his kingdom's business. We must share our substance with joy and gladness. Wherever we put it, we should do it as though we are partners with God. We do not miss the mark if we begin with the Old Testament tithe, which, by implication, has the New Testament blessing. Say what you will, the cheerful, sacrificial giver is drawn closer to Christ. Our giving and our living are tied together. Our spiritual barometer and our giving barometer are related.

Third, God's people on mission will want the discipline of giving time specifically related to his kingdom's business. And we must see in this time spent something of significance, something which has meaning in the lives of people and in God's business.

It may mean that we will be involved with some cause or some project which helps hurting humanity, some cause which may not be popular in its appeal or have widespread approval. We must be willing to take risks for Christ's sake, be willing to be fools for him.

Again, God's people on mission will want to be so disciplined that at least once a week they will gather together with his people in corporate worship. Going to church may be a habit, but it is one which if consistently neglected will result in spiritual regression and spiritual poverty.

Where this adventure of being on mission will take you, no one can tell you, but rest assured that God will have exciting experiences to offer you. There will be suffering for Christ's sake; there will be cost, but there will be joy and fullness of life that can come in no other way. To be joined in comradeship with a group of God's people who are really on mission for him can be the most exciting experience one can have. To feel the power of the prayers and to know the loving acceptance of such a group can fit one for victorious living and for sacrificial service.

To be open to God's direction; to listen with others for the voice of his Spirit to guide; to be ready to risk failure in his name; to lay it on the line for Christ's sake—this is living, and this is our mission.

"You are a chosen race, a royal priesthood, a holy nation, God's own people, that you may declare the wonderful deeds of him who called you out of darkness into his marvelous light."

AIDS TO WORSHIP

Hymns: "Jesus Calls Us"
"Take My Life, and Let It Be Consecrated"
Scripture: I Pet. 2:9-10

A Prayer

God, make me an instrument of your peace; where there is hatred, let me sow love; where there is injury, pardon; where there is doubt, faith; where there is despair, hope; where there is darkness, light; and where there is sadness, joy. O Divine Master, grant that I may not so much seek to be consoled as to console; to be understood as to understand; to be loved as to love; for it is in giving that we receive, it is in pardoning that we are pardoned, and it is in dying that we are born to eternal life. *Amen.*[1]

---

[1] Francis of Assisi.

God Is Already There

The late Dr. William Temple, Archbishop of Canterbury, once said that the "sermon is putting a light to the kindling which has already been laid for the fire." He is saying in effect that the seed of the Gospel is already in the human heart, that God is already at work, that this is his world and we are his children.

Long ago Augustine wrote, "Thou hast made us for Thyself, and our hearts are restless until they rest in Thee." This is another way of saying that "we are homesick for God, from whom we come, and for whom we have been made." On every hand today we see this homesickness of the soul for God. It is given expression in the mad rush men make for happiness and pleasure, many times caught in a round of meaningless activity. The outward actions of people indicate that there is a great need for an inward adventure which would add meaning and purpose to life.

God is at work planting within the human heart seeds of truth, and what is needed is that these seeds should be stimulated to flower. Or as William Temple put it, the kindling has already been laid; what is needed is a spark to ignite it, a light to start the fire.

We all need to be awakened, and to respond to the Gospel that is within us, to the truth that has been planted, to life as it really is. Man is haunted today by a destructive sense of guilt. He is conscious of his sins but too often not of his redemption. He is haunted by memories of what should have been, and he needs to find Him who can redeem.

Ernest Gordon, Dean of Princeton Chapel, said that memory needs to be awakened. But the memory of a man on his own is alienation—he is a stranger in a far country. God has already laid in our hearts his word of truth, but it must be kindled. The spoken word of God through the sermon brings memory into power for the one who hears. God is one who acts in history, and the Gospels were written that we might remember what he has done. They were written by people who were there. The preacher is able, if he is faithful to the Gospel, to give to the world what the world cannot give to itself—memory.

J. W. Stevenson in his remarkable book *God in My Unbelief* writes, "When I went to the succour of a brother I was never coming there first; I was always taking the little I had where God was giving His all. When I prayed it was always for one in whom God was already at work. When I went to speak Christ's word I went as an interpreter of what He was already saying within; I did not break new ground."

He tells how Dr. Christopher, an old minister, had gone south to London to seek for his son who had dishonored his home and left father and mother, keeping silent about what had become of him. "There was no address to guide him. Only after many days was the name of the street discovered; and when the old minister, with his white hair, stood at the end of it he knew it was beyond him to go from door to door of its length. But a street musician came by just then and

Dr. Christopher stopped him. Did he know an old air, one that had been a favorite in the manse when the children were young? Would he walk with him along the street as he played? And he told him why.

"So they went slowly, the street musician and the old minister with his hat in his hand so that his face could be seen, taking this last slender chance to find where his son was who had no use for him, seeking him who had no understanding of the love in his father's heart."[1]

This is what we need! Someone to remind us, to awaken our memories, to ignate the kindling already laid by God, to call us home again. Indeed, O God, "Thou hast made us for Thyself, and our hearts are restless until they rest in Thee."

AIDS TO WORSHIP

Hymns: "Breathe on Me, Breath of God"
"Savior, Like a Shepherd Lead Us"
Scripture: Isa. 40:28-31

A Prayer

O Thou, Who art the Light of the minds that know Thee, the Life of the souls that love Thee, and the Strength of the thoughts that seek Thee; help us so to know Thee, that we may truly love Thee, and so to love Thee that we may fully serve Thee, Whose service is perfect freedom; through Jesus Christ our Lord. *Amen.*[2]

---

[1] (London: Collins, Sons & Co., 1960).
[2] Gelasian Sacramentary.

A Committed Christian

"Am I a committed Christian?" This is the question! To what am I committed? What does it mean to be a Christian? What difference should it make in my life and my attitudes?

John J. Vincent in *Christ and Methodism* says that "a Christian is a man who somehow or other shows Christ to be his Lord. . . . Christianity is the body of attitudes and actions which perpetuates the pattern of Christ on earth."

In this definition of a Christian as a man who somehow or other shows Christ to be his Lord is a note that is lacking in so much of modern church life today. It is the note of obedience. It is the note of commitment to Christ. It has to do with discipline. How basic this is. Dr. Edward W. Bauman says that before Jesus talks about faith and trust, he talks about obedience.

In the Old Testament, Jeremiah reminds his people: "But this command I gave them, 'Obey my voice, and I will be your God, and you shall be my people; and walk in all the way that I command you, that it may be well with you'" (7:23). In the New Testament the same note of obedience is sounded. In Matt. 7:24 we find these words: "Every one then who hears these words of mine and does them will be like a wise man who built his house upon the rock." In John 10:27 we read these words: "My sheep hear my voice, and I know them, and they follow me."

The centurion recognized in Jesus one who commanded authority. Obedience is another way of finding faith; it gives structure to our faith.

In our Communion service we have these words: "And here we offer and present unto thee, O Lord, ourselves, our souls and bodies, to be a reasonable, holy, and living sacrifice unto thee." These are the words of the Christian who gives himself in complete surrender to Christ, who asks that He take all as a sacrifice to be used in His service. It is the word of the creature turning over to the Creator all that has been given, asking that it be spent in the Creator's service. It is a recognition that we do not own ourselves, but are owned of God.

Unfortunately, our generation does not think of the Christian faith or the church in terms of obedience. In fact, the Christian church is one of the easiest institutions to join today. Too many of us are halfhearted followers of our Lord. Too many of us are fair-weather Christians. Too many of us give him only the remnants—the leftovers—of our time and talent.

The committed Christian will have the conviction that Jesus' way is the only way. If the world is to feel the impact of the Gospel, we who call ourselves "followers of the way" surely need to be more convincing in our faith. If we do not believe wholeheartedly in the way of love, how can we expect a mad, revengeful world to believe in it. If our love is not undergirded with basic justice, it is mere sentimentality.

Let us go back anew to the records and discover the power of love in human life. From every page of the New Testament comes the testimony that the things about which Jesus talked and for which he died are real and life is not worthwhile without them. Men today are beginning to suspect that this is true, as all other theories have failed.

A committed Christian will come to see that the church exists to minister, not to be ministered to, and to give itself for the sake of the world. Mission to the world—this is our calling. We are to take his healing and saving message to the world, near and far. We are to come in to worship that we might go out to serve. Enter to worship—depart to serve. The church should be transforming, rather than being transformed by, the world in which it lives.

L. D. Johnson puts it like this:

"Too much of the time the church is not a recruiting and training station for soldiers engaged in a struggle of eternal consequence, but a combination kindergarten and old folks home. From such an atmosphere creative and productive people flee.

"As a pastor I confess with shame and sorrow that many of our members use the church as a convenience only. They pay their dues and expect the church to be there when its services are wanted. After all, the chapel is a lovely place for a wedding!

"From its preaching we do not take our convictions, but are angry if it preaches something that questions judgments we have learned from the world. . . .

"As a church member am I willing to be inconvenienced? Will I endure hardship for the sake of Christ? Will I tolerate being upset, disturbed, challenged? Am I prepared to make sacrifices, or do I want mainly to be patted on the back and told that I am a good guy?

"These are the questions we must face as Christians. And we must face them in light of the disillusionment of today's youth with institutional religion.

"In droves they are vacating the churches. A prominent American educator has declared that perhaps no more than two per cent of this generation's college students has any deep commitment to the church. Let us hope that he is too pessimistic.

"What is the mission of today's church? It is first of all the conversion of the church herself. How can the church tell the world that God's love redeems if there is such little evidence of redemption in the church?" [1]

Paul Tournier writes with penetrating insight: "Even in our world today, deeply pagan as it is, every man can have a totally new experience as soon as he allows God to direct his real life and not merely to inspire his feelings. A new civilization will not spring full-grown from the brain of some theoretician. It will be built through bold obedience of countless Christians." [2]

To be sure, these are difficult days, days that demand daring and obedient disciples. But with such

---

[1] The *Greenville* (S.C.) *News,* January 2, 1966.

[2] *The Whole Person in a Broken World,* trans. John and Helen Doberstein (New York: Harper & Row, 1964), p. 167.

discipleship will come renewal of the church and a changed world.

Louis Clinton Wright has said, "A spiritually defeated world needs to know that a rugged faith in God still makes it possible to say, 'If any man be in Christ, he is a new creature.'"

AIDS TO WORSHIP

Hymns: "Dear Lord and Father of Mankind"
"O Jesus, I Have Promised"
Scripture: Matt. 7:13-28

A Prayer

O Jesus Christ, the Lord of all good life, who hast called us to help build the city of God; do thou enrich and purify our lives and deepen in us our discipleship. Help us daily to know more of thee, and through us by the power of thy Spirit, show forth thyself to other men. Make us humble, brave and loving; make us ready for adventure. We do not ask that thou wilt keep us safe, but that thou wilt keep us loyal; who for us didst face death unafraid, and dost live and reign with the Father and the Holy Spirit, God for ever and ever. *Amen.*[3]

---

[3] *Prayers New and Old,* Forward Movement Publications.

The Dark Night of the Soul

Georgia Harkness has written a book entitled *The Dark Night of the Soul*. This title suggests the plight of many a soul in our generation when despair faces mankind, when darkness hovers over the earth, when personal affairs disintegrate, when the future is unpredictable, when the task ahead seems too heavy for the strength at hand.

Who of us has not faced the dark night of the soul, when the bottom seemed to have dropped out, when the course ahead seemed blocked? What are we to say to these low moods, these disturbing moments, these dark nights?

For the background of our thought let us turn to the experience of the prophet Jeremiah when his world was filled with darkness, when he was called to carry a light in a dark night. Raymond Calkins in *The Romance of the Ministry* illuminates Jeremiah's experience.

Jeremiah was then a young man living in Anathoth when God called him to the task of bearing a message of judgment to his own people, whom he loved. He brooded over it. What a job it was! How inadequate he felt to fulfill it! He saw clearly the corruption of the nation and the immorality of the people. And the more he thought about it, the more depressed he became.

But then he began to reason with himself, reminding himself that it was God who called him to such a task. It was God who had spoken. What must he do? As he walked along, he said, "Ah, God, I cannot speak in public. Who am I to go before such a group? They will not listen to my voice. How can I stand against such evil and make men hear my message?"

The whole countryside lent a hand in adding to his depression. It was in the bleak of winter. All foliage had disappeared. A cold stillness gripped the air. Nowhere could he see any sign of life. Then suddenly in the midst of this barren land he saw something which made light come into his eyes. In the midst of his despairing thoughts, in the midst of his hopelessness, he lifted his eyes and beheld the sight of an almond tree breaking forth into bloom.

It was just one rod, sheltered by a bank from the wintry winds, that had blossomed forth in beauty. But that was enough for him, for this became a reminder to him that God was alive, that all was not lost. The bloom of the almond in Palestine is the first harbinger of spring. Yes, it became a sign of spring, a touch of color in the bleakness. He knew that within a few weeks the whole countryside would be covered with blooms.

That was all that he wanted to know. For the rod of the almond tree became for Jeremiah a reminder that God was alive and at work in his world; that in spite of the coldness of winter, summer was on its way. And in the strength of that assurance that God was alive, was working, Jeremiah went forth to answer God's call and to become his messenger. He went in the faith that there was an unseen power at work, that God was guiding him all along the way. The bloom of the almond became a symbol for him that remained real in the long years ahead and always drove him forward to his tasks in confidence. What does this tell us?

It tells us that when we face the dark night of our souls, we need this sign of the almond tree. We need it today. God is saying to us today as he did to Jeremiah, "No, all is not lost. There is hope, for I am at work! I am still in command. Even though the clouds of discouragement hang low they shall be blown away, and sunshine shall come again to bathe the earth in all its healing powers." Yes, the affairs of life can be bad, but they are not all bad. Always in life there is the rod of the almond tree, the promise of new life and energy beneath what seems to be barrenness.

The sign that we need today is one that men found in the past that could be depended upon. Men who have wrought valiantly for God have been those who have kept faith in the rod of the almond tree.

Raymond Calkins calls attention to Paul, who kept this faith. "All winter," said the men of wisdom in Greece and Rome, concerning the slaves who had lived so long in subserviance. "No," said Paul, "I see the rod of the almond tree." So in the face of unspeakable odds he carried the message of Christ to them. Even into Caesar's household the message went and captured men's hearts and turned the Roman would upside down. Paul was secure in the faith that no man labors in vain who labors in the Lord, and that "the seeds of the gospel have within it a glorious immortality."

There is a story of a young Scottish minister who was transferred from his quiet country parish to a city church in Glasgow. He was standing on the bridge spanning the Clyde, in a dejected mood surveying the dark and grimy outlines of the city, when Thomas Chalmers, the eminent Scottish preacher, passed by, saw the young man, and understood his mood. Chalmers put his arm around him and pointed to the city saying, "Grand field of operations, that." He saw the rod of the almond tree.

However dark may appear the winter, let us never forget that springtime is not far off. When we become discouraged, let us never forget that God's energies are at work silently but powerfully for righteousness and peace. After we have surveyed the field, let us not leave out of our calculations the spiritual forces which join hands with us in the task.

AIDS TO WORSHIP

Hymns: "A Mighty Fortress Is Our God"
"Lead On, O King Eternal"
Scripture: Isa. 40:1-11

A Prayer

O God of Light, Father of Life, Giver of Wisdom, Benefactor of our souls, who givest to the fainthearted who put their trust in Thee those things into which the angels desire to look; O Sovereign Lord, who hast brought us up from the depths of darkness to light, who hast given us life from death, who hast graciously bestowed upon us freedom from slavery, and what hast scattered the darkness of sin within us; do Thou now also enlighten the eyes of our understanding, and sanctify us wholly in soul, body and spirit. *Amen.*[1]

---

[1] Liturgy of St. Mark.

Refuse to Pity Yourself

The other day a lady who has had sorrow come into her life said to me, "I refuse to pity myself. People do not want to be around a person who is sorry for herself."

I have thought a great deal about what she said and know that she is right. Pity only adds to our sorrow and misery. It is luxury we cannot afford. It focuses attention upon ourselves and prolongs the anguish of loneliness and grief.

Of course there are a lot of things in life which tempt us to give in to pity. No one of mature years can escape the hazards of life which engender pity. Misfortune, sorrow, illness, abuse, cruelty, loneliness, disappointment—all these are grounds for complaint. As long as we live in a world like ours—which I do believe is the best kind of world for the purpose of God—we will have reason to be sorry for ourselves.

The faithlessness of a wife, the thoughtlessness of a husband, the waywardness of a daughter—these give cause for concern. The alcoholic brings tears to many a home. Then there is lingering illness. There is pain and death. There is the tragedy of accident. There is financial distress. There is business failure.

We should never assume that life can always be a bed of roses. With the fragrant flower goes the thorn. The bitter is mingled with the sweet. Unwanted circumstances must be accepted as part of life's experiences.

It is not that God is malicious and unkind in making a world like ours where these things exist. He is merciful, and the possibility of evil and pain is but part of his plan. We do not know why this has to be, but we do know that man grows only by overcoming, by withstanding, by facing the winter winds of life. It may be that this is God's way of developing character in his children.

Sometimes when we are tempted to pity ourselves, we should just look around and see the plight of others. We should go to a hospital and walk up and down the halls, see there suffering and sorrow as well as rejoicing and renewed health; see there bedfast patients who are able to smile, the incurably sick who have no complaint. We can see there how "tribulation worketh patience; and patience, experience; and experience, hope" (KJV). Regardless of our lot, there are others in company with us.

But what about pity? What is its antidote? It is gratitude.

So, when we feel sorry for ourselves, let us determine to face the future in the spirit of gratitude rather than grievance. Be thankful! Be grateful! "Count your many blessings, name them one by one." Let us thank God for the little things of life: a lovely flower, a singing bird, frost on the housetop, the patter of rain, the glow of a sunset, the laughter of a child. Be grateful for the aroma of good coffee. Delight in friendship. Be thankful for sleep. And when we cannot sleep, let us be thankful that we can talk with God. Taking life not for granted, but in gratitude brings abiding joy and drives away pity and self-concern.

And when life has been broken by sorrow and disappointment, it can be mended and put together again by the cheerful heart. As Proverbs puts it: "A cheerful heart is a good medicine." A cheerful heart is a happy heart, and a happy heart is a grateful heart!

With Shakespeare let us say, "O Lord, who lends me life, lend me a heart replete with thankfulness."

AIDS TO WORSHIP

Hymns: "Rise Up, O Men of God"
"This Is My Father's World"
Scripture: Psa. 118:1-24

A Prayer

Almighty God, unto whom all hearts are open, all desires known, and from whom no secrets are hid: Cleanse the thoughts of our hearts by the inspiration of thy Holy Spirit, that we may perfectly love thee, and worthily magnify thy holy name; through Christ our Lord. *Amen.*[1]

---

[1] *The Book of Common Prayer.*

Maintaining a Sense of Wonder

The Hayden Planetarium in New York once advertised that it would take reservations for trips to the moon as well as to Venus, Mars, Jupiter, and Saturn. The trip to the moon, covering 240,000 miles, would take only nine and a half hours in one of the interplanetary planes.

In the spirit of jest, prospective travelers were warned that this speed would be hard on the blood pressure, and that the moon was a cold spot covered with a thick layer of powdered pumice, where locomotion would be difficult and conversation impossible.

Nevertheless, in spite of these drawbacks over 18,000 reservations poured in within a few days. The letters were studied by a psychologist. Discounting the obvious gags, like letters from children who wanted a hot-dog concession, most of the letters came from people who seemed tired of it all. They wanted a chance to get away from their own troubles.

One woman from Massachusetts wrote: "It would be heaven to get away from this busy earth. I honestly wish God would let me get away . . . and just go somewhere where it's nice and peaceful, good, safe and secure."

One reason for man's desire to get away from it all is a lost sense of wonder. When a man ceases to wonder, he loses his zest for living. When we take

MAINTAINING A SENSE OF WONDER

so much in life for granted, we come perilously close to losing a deep interest in living.

One of the most profound nursery rhymes is one we all know:

> Twinkle, twinkle little star,
> *How I wonder what you are!*
> Up above the world so high,
> Like a diamond in the sky.

It is this childhood wondering that Jesus was thinking of when he placed a little child in the midst of the disciples and called him the greatest of all. He must have been thinking of children's questing minds when he said that "to such belongs the kingdom of heaven."

A little child is filled with a sense of wonder. All around him are things to wonder about. Everything holds something for him to discover. What a glorious world this is to him!

And it is true that when we cease to wonder, God's secrets remain unrevealed. In every area of living this is true.

The psalmist writes of it in Psalm 119: "Open my eyes, that I may behold wondrous things out of thy law."

In the book of Acts just after the lame man had been made to walk again, we read these words: "And all the people saw him walking and praising God, and recognized him as the one who sat for alms at the Beautiful Gate of the temple; and they were filled with wonder and amazement at what had happened to him."

"Open my eyes, that I may behold wondrous things out of thy law." ". . . filled with wonder and amazement." How we need to see life like this today.

What then are some of the things in life which should excite our sense of wonder?

In the first place, there is the wonder of God's world.

The psalmist looks at the world with glee: "The heavens are telling the glory of God; and the firmament proclaims his handiwork."

There is so much that is lovely in God's world. There is so much that is extra, just thrown in to add dazzling beauty. And how blind we are at times to it.

Earl Musselman was born blind and later received his sight. In an article in *The Christian Century* he gives his impressions of his new visible world:

"There are numberless things about my new world and its sighted inhabitants that perplex me. But most outstanding is the fact that so many of you are oblivious to all the beauty around you—colors, flowers, trees, fields, rivers, mountains, skies, sunsets, moonlight, and the sea and all the glories of nature that make our world a Garden of Eden. I cannot help but think that there is another kind of blindness almost as bad as that of the eyes—a blindness of the soul that keeps sighted people from really seeing and enjoying the beauty of nature."

The wonder of God's world. Let's open our eyes and see it.

In a book by Somerset Maugham, *Of Human Bondage,* we have a picture of a youth who had apparently failed. "The Vicar looked up at his nephew: 'Then these last two years may be regarded as so much wasted time?'"

"Philip reflected for an instant: 'I don't know about that. I learned one or two useful things. I learned to look at hands, which I'd never looked at before. And instead of just looking at houses and trees, I learned to look at houses and trees against the sky. And I learned also that shadows are not black but colored.'"

In the second place, there is the wonder of God's children living in his world.

Have you ever looked with wonder at a human being? Look at the human heart, for example.

It weighs only ten ounces—little more than half a pound—yet we are told that this little pump, the size of your fist, sends out six ounces of blood at each contraction.

In other words every twenty-four hours it pumps up to five thousand gallons, or twenty tons, of blood. And when those twenty-four hours are filled with excessive stress, the heart may propel as much as fifty to a hundred tons of blood.

Wonderful body. Dr. Alexis Carrel in his book *Man, the Unkown* said that "Blood carries to each tissue the proper nourishment, but acts, at the same time, as a sewer that takes away the waste products set free by living tissues. It also contains chemical substances and cells capable of repairing organs wherever necessary."

Wonderful body! But greater than the body is the soul which it houses. Made in the image of God, we are children of God. We can climb to heights of nobility. We can love. We can build. We can sacrifice. Wonderful soul!

The wonder of who you are! The real you, encrusted with fears and worry, with antagonism and bitterness, with envy and jealousy, the real you needs to be set free. The real you is a wonder to behold. God has made you in his own image, and this image will shine through if we can set it free.

Love yourself for what you really are. Be glad you are you—the only one of your kind that God has made. Never despise yourself, but be grateful to God that he made you and pray that he will help to set you free from all that would keep you from being yourself.

Accept yourself—the real you—knowing that you are a wonderful creation, made to love and to be loved, to labor, to create, to achieve, to forgive, to trust.

Accept yourself—the real you—knowing that no apology is needed for who you are or what you are, for God made you to be loving and to be free.

Accept yourself—the real you—in the circumstances in which you find yourself, knowing that God will labor with you to help you be your best where you are.

Accept yourself—the real you—knowing that you are

never alone, that God is the source of your being and concerned in every affair of your life.

Accept yourself—the real you—knowing that you are a lovable creature and that you can be free from all that makes you unloving.

Be grateful that God meant for you to love and to accept yourself. Be glad you are you, and thank him for making you.

The wonder of who you are!

O the wonder of such love—God's love. Will you not respond to such love by giving your love in return?

AIDS TO WORSHIP

Hymns: "Awake, Awake to Love and Work"
"This Is My Father's World"
Scripture: Psalm 24

A Prayer

Lord God Almighty, Shaper and Ruler of all creatures, we pray for thy great mercy to guide us to thy will, to make our minds steadfast, to strengthen us against temptation, to put far from us all unrighteousness. Shield us against our foes, seen and unseen. Teach us so that we may inwardly love thee before all things with a clean mind and a clean body, for thou art our Maker and our Redeemer, our Trust and our Hope. *Amen.*[1]

---

[1] King Alfred's Prayer.

Being Renewed Every Day

The other day I was in the home of a friend of many years. It has been over a year since she lost the companion of her life. They were devoted to each other and had been married well over fifty years. Of course, there has been a real adjustment for this dear lady, but even though she is over eighty, she carries on in a noble and remarkable way.

She reached for her Bible and told me that recently she had come upon the most magnificent verse, which has really become her own, and by which she lives every day. It is found in II Cor. 4:16, and I, too, commend it to you: "So we do not lose heart. Though our outer nature is wasting away, our inner nature is being renewed every day."

"This," she said, "is what I live by now, and how wonderful God has been to me. He has given me special strength since Uncle Jack left me."

Then without the least sign of emotion, she told me that she has planned her funeral in detail. She has selected those who are to serve as her pallbearers. She has picked out the dress she wants to wear. She then said, "Now here is a poem I want you to read."

> Sunset and evening star,
>   And one clear call for me!

And may there be no moaning of the bar,
  When I put out to sea,

But such a tide as moving seems asleep,
  Too full for sound and foam,
When that which drew from out the boundless
    deep
Turns again home.

Twilight and evening bell,
  And after that the dark!
And may there be no sadness of farewell,
  When I embark;

For tho' from out our bourne of Time and
    Place
  The flood may bear me far,
I hope to see my Pilot face to face
  When I have crost the bar.[1]

Hers is a faith that is unwavering and that sustains her in these sunset years of life. She still teaches in Sunday school and is interested in all that concerns her church. She has tried to retire from her duties several times, but the church urges her to continue.

After my wife and I left her that day, we stopped by to see another senior citizen. He has had a marvelous life and is known the world over as one of this century's most gifted authors. He will be remembered as a great literary figure and a Christian gentleman.

I showed him this verse, II Cor. 4:16. He com-

[1] Tennyson, "Crossing the Bar."

mented on its meaning and its beauty, and said that daily he marvels at his clearness of mind and alertness of mental vigor, even though his outer nature is wearing thin. He has his good days and bad, and this was one of his better days, physically. What insight this man has, and what beauty of expression! It is always a source of inspiration to visit him and his gracious wife.

I leave this verse with you.

"So we do not lose heart. Though our outer nature is wasting away, our inner nature is being renewed every day."

AIDS TO WORSHIP

Hymns: "Come, Ye That Love the Lord"
"Holy Spirit, Faithful Guide"
Scripture: II Cor. 4:7-16

A Prayer

O Lord our God, who art always more ready to bestow thy good gifts upon us than we are to seek them, and art willing to give more than we desire or deserve: Help us so to seek that we may truly find, so to ask that we may joyfully receive, so to knock that the door of thy mercy may be opened unto us. *Amen.*[2]

---

[2] Book of Common Order, St. Giles' Cathedral, Edinburgh.

And We Are Whole Again

We all want to be better than we are, to learn how to live best with ourselves and with others, and deep down we want to learn how to relate ourselves to God. When we learn these secrets, we have wholeness of life.

Someone has well said that life is a landscaping job. We have been given a site with contours, with possibilities, with limitations, with general outlines, many of which are beyond our control. Our job is to take the site and see what we can do with it. This is what Studdert-Kennedy had in mind in saying, "When we come to the end of the way, God will ask, 'Well, what did you make of it?'"

Paul has a word for us here, found in II Cor. 5:17: "Therefore if any man be in Christ, he is a new creature; old things are passed away; behold all things are become new." He is saying that any man who is bound closely to Christ will be radically transformed from his old sinful state. The old state of perverted outlook resulting too often from an all-too-human point of view passes away. "Behold," he says, "all things become new" He declares that in Christian faith, fellowship, and service for Christ a new and right relationship to God and life comes.

To be in Christ, Paul is saying, means that an inner change takes place which is equivalent to a new creation. One is not merely improved, reformed, or altered, but he is remade. As someone has said, "He is different from what he was at his best. The old has passed away . . . the new has come.

"The old may refer to the desires and purposes of the self-centered life, and the new to the desires and purposes of the Christ-centered life."

Let us look at this experience.

In the first place, when we confront Christ we are attracted to him on the one hand and disconcerted by him on the other. We feel his magnitude and magnetism. We are awed by his life and sacrifice. We are lured by his teaching, and have a deep, indwelling feeling that life is as he said. There is something within us that lures us toward him.

And yet, on the other hand, we feel that with the stain of sin coloring our lives he is unapproachable and irrelevant to our daily affairs. Fastened as we are to the way of the world, we conclude that all his teaching is exalted idealism.

But when we look closer and enter the portals of the Christian faith, thank God, we find that what Jesus was talking about is vitally relevant to our common life. We come to see squarely that he was thinking of people like us and the needs of our feeble lives. His message, his gospel is for people who fall and need to be lifted, people stained by sin, who need cleansing. The gospel does not forget the ordinary realities of our lives. It is designed neither for supermen nor dreamers, but for plain people like ourselves in need of a Savior.

Beginning with stories of people in the Old Testament and continuing through Paul's picture of the Christian community, our Bible portrays in vivid, striking form the human frailties of men. It is difficult to think of a vice that is not mentioned in the Bible, and it is precisely to people bound down with such human weakness that God speaks. It is for persons like ourselves that Jesus came. Relevant? God's concern and plan for men is the most relevant and realistic fact of life. If we doubt whether the Gospel has the answer for our petty, small dimensions, our answer, as Visser 't Hooft says, "comes from the publicans and sinners, from Zacchaeus and Mary Magdalene, and even from Peter who denied his Master."

When we find ourselves burdened by the weight of a thousand failures and in need of courage to carry on in spite of our constant defeats, Jesus speaks to us not only of following an example, but also of newness of life and the grace of God.

In the second place, when we are in Christ we find strength for life's loads. Jesus says, "I have food to eat of which ye do not know. . . . My food is to do the will of him who sent me." Here Jesus is speaking of spiritual food, which even brings nourishment to tired muscles and fatigued bodies. It was a plus, an over-and-above which saw him through. It was a reserve ready for tapping in hours of need. Doing God's will became food and meat. It took from his life its strain and stress and brought order, peace, and poise.

How we need this today! We are torn and twisted by conflicting voices. Demands are crowding in upon us. Inwardly we are tornadoes. Outwardly we are nerves on edge. We need dreadfully one Purpose, one Will, one Life, one Voice to follow, making all else fit together. Following His purpose for our lives is the only way to be whole. God made us for himself and inwardly we are restless until we rest in him.

Medical science is now discovering what Jesus proclaimed long ago, that inner peace has a profound effect upon the physical well-being of a person. We read that Jesus healed many sick of body by his touch upon their lives. "And he healed many that were sick of divers diseases, and cast out many devils." (Mark 1:34.)

The same thing is true today. A life that is at peace with God is at peace not only with men but also with itself. *The British Medical Journal* says: "There is not a tissue in the human body wholly removed from the influence of the spirit."

Jesus went about teaching, preaching, healing, redeeming the mind, soul, and body. Pausing in his presence, listening to his voice, reading from his Word, following his will, all these bring order, poise, wholeness to these lives of ours.

No wonder then that many men who seem to have outgrown religion return to church to find that Presence in worship that can bind up their wounds, heal their hurts, and make them whole again. In Christ we find a power that "enables us to endure the stress of what cannot be altered, to eliminate what can be vanquished, and to find fellowship with a living Presence, that makes us know we labor, live, and laugh not alone."

AIDS TO WORSHIP

Hymns: "All Hail the Power of Jesus' Name"
"O Master, Let Me Walk with Thee"
Scripture: II Cor. 5:16-21

A Prayer

Almighty and everlasting God, in whom we live and move and have our being, who hast created us for thyself, so that our hearts are restless until they find rest in thee: Grant unto us such purity of heart and strength of purpose, that no selfish passion may hinder us from knowing thy will, and no weakness from doing it. In thy light may we see life clearly, and in thy service find perfect freedom; through Jesus Christ our Lord. *Amen.*[1]

---

[1] John Watson.

The Story of a Prayer

It was a bleak January morning in 1956. The New Year had just heralded another allotment of time, and I was facing major surgery. To say that I wasn't concerned is to tamper with the truth, for before me was an operation that would last five hours. Doctors and nurses had assured me that all was in order, and that all would be well. Family and friends had encouraged me, but still it was not the way I would have liked to start the New Year.

Then, a letter came just before I was to go into the operating room. It was from a college friend I had not seen in many years. The contents of that letter brought strength and comfort to me, as well as a surprise. His letter read in part:

"It's been nearly twenty-five years now since I have seen you, but I have heard about you and your work in mysterious ways. Once during World War II when I was recuperating from wounds in a hospital near Bromsgrove, England, I saw one of your prayers in a Methodist publication, *The Upper Room*, I believe. I was so impressed that I copied it." (The prayer was written out in full.)

A Morning Prayer

O God, for another day, for another morning, for another hour, for another minute, for another chance to live and serve Thee, I am truly grateful. Do Thou this day free me:

From fear of the future;
From anxiety of the morrow;
From bitterness toward anyone;
From cowardice in face of danger;
From laziness in face of work;
From failure before opportunity;
From weakness when Thy power is at hand.
But fill me with:
Love that knows no barrier;
Courage that cannot be shaken;
Faith strong enough for the darkness;
Strength sufficient for my tasks;
Loyalty to Thy Kingdom's goal;
Wisdom to meet life's complexities;
Power to lift men unto Thee.
Be Thou with me for another day and use me as Thou wilt; in Christ's name, I pray. *Amen.*[1]

The letter continued, "Seeing a prayer like that by someone I knew when I was alone and ill and far away from home, meant more to me than I was able to put into words. I have used that prayer . . . on a number of occasions since. All who heard it have gained strength but not quite in the same intimate way as I because I had a spiritual communion through you not available to the others."

I tell this story because at the moment I received that letter from my engineer friend something from

---

[1] July-August-September, 1944. Copyright 1944 by *The Upper Room* and used with permission.

DEVOTIONS FOR PERSONAL AND GROUP RENEWAL

the past reached out to sustain me. The words of my own prayer came back as though to become again my prayer for an hour of real need. The promises of Ecclesiastes became real, "Cast your bread upon the waters; for you will find it after many days."

But this instance concerning "A Morning Prayer" is one of many that have come to me. Following its publication on the back cover of *The Upper Room*, it was published in a card series of prayers and poems and distributed by *The Upper Room*. One manufacturer secured them for his employees who numbered in the thousands. Don McNeill included it in his book *Twenty Years of Memory Time* comprising favorite readings on his Breakfast Club program from 1933 through 1951.

One day I received a letter from a lady in California who had had this prayer printed in a little leaflet for personal distribution. She said it had meant so much to her that she wanted to share its sentiment with others. Another lady told of how she had pasted it on her mirror, and how every morning it became her prayer for the day.

A minister friend during World War II was wounded in France, and while he was out on the battlefield waiting to be carried to a hospital, his runner handed him the copy of *The Upper Room* that carried this prayer. He said it helped to strengthen him for the long hours and days of his recovery.

I tell this story, too, because I believe that this prayer in some mysterious way came to me many years ago during a period of meditation. I do believe that it just "wrote itself." It was a real prayer, written with no thought of publication or of being used by others. Thus, I know it is authentic. Whatever merit it may have, and whatever help it brings to others, lies in this authenticity. I was merely used as an instrument to record it.

AIDS TO WORSHIP

Hymns: "O For a Faith that will Not Shrink"
"Guide Me, O Thou Great Jehovah"
Scripture: Heb. 11:1-10

A Prayer

Almighty God, who hast sent the Spirit of truth unto us to guide into all truth: So rule our lives by thy power that we may be truthful in thought and word and deed. Arm us with such trust in the truth that is invisible, that we may ask no rest from its demands and have no fear in its service; through Jesus Christ our Lord. *Amen.*[2]

---

[2] Bishop Wescott.

We Need a Stalwart Faith

On every hand men across the world are in despair. They are seeing as men in the past have seen that no amount of scientific invention, nor elaborate world organization, nor plea for good will, nor authority of church or state, separate or combined, is adequate for solving the individual and social problems of the day. As in days past men today are beginning to feel that the answers lie in the resources of a vital spiritual religion.

Surely it takes a more vital religion today to mend and rebuild this shattered world.

If religion today is to measure up in meeting the distress of this modern world, there must be a recovery of faith in a living God. To be sure many today believe in the idea of God, that he must exist somewhere, that more than likely he made this universe. But far too few of us have a vital faith in a living God, whose will we must find and follow or life is lost. There are some who think of him as an absentee landlord, one who is responsible for our creation, but who has left off being active in life; one who is transcendent and has no relationship with us. But the church will recover a rugged faith only as it places at its center, God. Only faith in the God of Jesus as a loving father active in the affairs of men will reconstruct personality for triumphant living in a day like this.

Sherwood Eddy once said, "Faith is not believing something irrational; it is doing something for God regardless of consequences." What are you doing for God today? Are you consciously following his will? Well might we review again the Baptismal Covenant, "Will you then obediently keep God's holy will and commandments?" Answering that question affirmatively only will bring to us a vital and living religion. History attests to the fact that nothing but faith in God will direct the motives of men to do right regardless of the consequences. We need to hear personally the words "Thus saith the Lord" if we are to go straight in a crooked world.

Louis Clinton Wright has said, "A spiritually defeated world needs to know that a rugged faith in God still makes it possible to say, 'If any man be in Christ he is a new creature.'" Only as we recover this New Testament truth can our religion become dynamic.

A second priority to a rugged faith is an urgent concern for man's lostness—his sin. Too many of us in the modern church have stricken from our vocabulary the word *sin.* "Nice" people in our "nice" congregations do not like to hear their pastors speak of their sin, and so many pastors, desiring to please, omit it. Recently, a graduate from a high school in Washington returned for his fiftieth anniversary and said of the city that very little had changed except preachers' sermons and ladies' hats. "The preachers," he said, "no longer preach 'hot sermons.'" Surely we preachers don't want to go back to a time like the day when Jonathan Edwards preached a sermon in a New England church on "Sinners in the Hands of an Angry God," and following it several people fainted out of fear. But pew and pulpit alike must rediscover the reality of sin in the world and in themselves, or else our religion will remain pale and fruitless.

A third rugged element essential to a virile Christianity is a renewed conviction that Jesus' way is the only way. In A. J. Cronin's novel *The Keys of the Kingdom* he portrays the life of a devout Catholic priest whose goodness and daily exemplification of Christ captured the heart of a thoughtful Chinese nobleman. After many years of testing, Mr. Chia comes to Father Chisholm and says, "Once, many years ago, when you cured my son, I was not serious [that is about becoming a Christian]. But then I was unaware of the nature of your life . . . of its patience, quietness, and courage. The goodness of religion is best judged by the goodness of its adherents. My friend—you have conquered me by example." [1]

Finally, one other essential we need is a stalwart faith. We must rediscover or discover for ourselves the presence of the living Christ. It is not enough to have faith in a living God, we must know him personally through his living revelation, Christ. We need more than a concern for man's sin, we must of neces-

[1] (Boston: Little, Brown & Co., 1941), p. 320.

sity have an experience with one who is able to forgive sins. To believe only in Jesus' way of life leaves us without power unless we also come into vital relationship with his ever-present spirit. Somehow we must find this, or else our faith is barren. We have depended too long upon our human achievements, important as they are, for our salvation and have neglected even in the church the One who through a life-giving experience is able to make us over and send us out singing. The words that he left with us must be taken literally: "And I will pray the Father, and he shall give you another Comforter, that he may abide with you for ever" (John 14:16 KJV).

The Christ is more real today than when he walked the hills of ancient Palestine. His presence is closer to men today than when he talked to them by the seashore. He is alive, and we must feel his power and presence with us if our religion is to be vibrant.

AIDS TO WORSHIP

Hymns: "I Love Thy Kingdom, Lord"
"Faith of Our Fathers"
Scripture: John 14:1-27

A Prayer

O Lord, our heavenly Father, we offer and present unto thee ourselves, our souls and bodies, to be a reasonable, holy, and living sacrifice unto thee. Take us as we are and make us more fit for thy service. Use us for thyself and for the edification of thy Church. We are not our own, but thine, bought with a price; therefore claim us as thy right, keep us as thy charge, and use us as thou wilt, to the glory of thy holy name and the good of our fellow men through Jesus Christ our Lord. *Amen.*[2]

---

[2] *The Book of Worship* (Nashville: The Methodist Publishing House, 1964).

Guidelines for Church Renewal

In the 1964 Discipline of The Methodist Church there is a resolution which was passed by the General Conference of that year. It is a resolution entitled, "Renewal for Witnessing." In the first paragraph we have these words:

The Church is of God and is the household of faith, but its spiritual energies ebb and flow. When the Church loses sight of its origin and destiny, the tide goes out. When its household duties obscure its mission, it stands in desperate need of renewal. The time for renewal has come. The call to mission is the hope of this renewal. In the recognition that "the Church exists for mission as a candle exists for burning" lies the promise of the resurrection of the Body of Christ in our time. Renewal is our most compelling imperative.[1]

Certainly no one can serve in the church today and not be disappointed with the shallow witness given in many areas of church life. It is estimated that only about one third of the members of the church are active: this is a general figure and varies from place to place. Roy A. Burkhart says that

the contemporary church is made up of millions of people who, like Joseph of Arimathea, are secret disciples with

[1] ¶ 1825, p. 688.

half-hearted loyalty. These persons want the Kingdom of God but do not want it first: the love of God is second to the love of power, money, security, and pleasure. The contemporary church in large majority is composed of persons who hold in their hearts a deep conviction that there is something greater in life than they are, something they call God. . . .

If all the half-loyalty and secret discipleship and the lukewarm fealty that are accorded to God were suddenly to flame into fiery, zealous devotion, this generation would save an imperiled civilization. There is less and less room today for secret and divided loyalties.[2]

Happily today there are rumblings of discontent and honest searching for new life and new vigor in the church. Many people feel that there must be more relationship between what we study and learn in church and the world around us. Many feel that we must turn the searchlight of God's truth in the church upon the great issues which face men today and that we must not be afraid to discuss controversial issues of our time.

To be in today's church and part of the movement searching for the answers to our time is an exciting adventure. To labor with those who sincerely want to know the truth and the way is an exciting adventure. To share in prayer groups with a cross section of people who lay bare their hearts and probe to find the mind of Christ as it relates to today's world, to feel the earnestness of their prayers as they pray, and to

[2] *The Person You Can Be* (New York: Harper & Row, 1962), p. 198.

watch them stand for the right, out where it is hard to stand, all this lifts one up. To see a growing concern among laymen and clergy alike that the gospel be relevant to daily life, that compassion reflect the spirit of Christ, and that the church minister to all men everywhere is a quickening experience.

H. Richard Niebuhr was looking at the church and its continual need to reform itself to meet the demands of the age in which it lives. In an article in *The Christian Century* he wrote:

> The immediate reformation of the church that I pray for, look for, and want to work for, in the time that may remain to me is its reformation not now by separation from the world, but by a new entrance into it without conformity to it. I believe our separation has gone far enough and that now we must find new ways of doing what we were created to do.

What then are some guidelines for church renewal today?

In the first place, renewal of the church today must be anchored in biblical faith, the Word of God. The church which finds a rebirth of spiritual power does so only as its members turn to the Scriptures as a record of God's saving activity. It is to see the Scriptures interpreted in terms of Christ, "for Christ is the Lord of the Scriptures," according to Martin Luther.

Luther observed that the message of Christ "is not simply an old song about an event that happened 1,500 years ago . . . ; it is a gift and bestowing that endures forever."

To be confronted with God's Word means that we must return to the reading of it as did our forebears of old. Daily we must let it speak to us, all in the spirit of Christ. Christ is our guide.

In the second place, renewal comes to the church when it sees its task as mission to the world. The church exists not to be ministered to, but to minister, to give itself for the sake of the world. We are to take his healing and saving message to the world, near and far. We are to come in to worship that we might go out to serve.

It is right that we talk with each other within the church concerning our faith, that we share the deepest experiences of our lives, but let us not limit our dialogue to the church. We are to carry on outside. The church should be transforming rather than being transformed by the world in which it lives.

Finally, renewal of the church will come when the community of faith makes room for the work of the Holy Spirit in its midst. The Holy Spirit seeks to renew and bless men in the faith—to bless all those who bear the name of Jesus Christ. It is through the Holy Spirit that Jesus Christ reaches out to us today. He is seeking to guide and to lead us in his way. After we have done all that we can, we must wait for the Spirit and be willing to follow his leading. Here God is seeking to reach out and get hold of us, and to help make us whole again.

It is the Holy Spirit who will open the door of prayer and make it more vital in our lives. It is the Holy Spirit who will move us to intercessory prayer, to go on errands for others in our prayers. It behooves us to be sure that we are not throttling the work of the Holy Spirit by the actions we take, or the attitudes we hold, or the indifference we may have. It is a terrible thing to try and block God and his purpose for life. God is at work in our midst through his Spirit.

AIDS TO WORSHIP

Hymns: "The Church's One Foundation"
"A Charge to Keep I Have"
Scripture: Eph. 3:14-21

A Prayer

O God our Father, we pray for thy Church, which is set today amid the perplexities of a changing order, and face to face with new tasks. Baptize her afresh in the life-giving spirit of Jesus! Bestow upon her a great responsiveness to duty, a swifter compassion with suffering, and an utter loyalty to the will of God. Help her to proclaim boldly the coming of the kingdom of God. Put upon her lips the ancient Gospel of her Lord. Fill her with the prophets' scorn and tyranny, and with a Christlike tenderness for the heavy-laden and downtrodden. Bid her cease from seeking her own life, lest she lose it. Make her valiant to give up her life to humanity, that, like her crucified Lord, she may mount by the path of the cross to a higher glory; through the same Jesus Christ our Lord. *Amen.*[3]

---

[3] Walter Rauschenbusch.

The Grace of God

Sometime ago a friend of mine was talking about words we often use in our religious vocabulary, and he singled out one which he would like discussed in a sermon. It is the word *grace*. We do use it over and over again in our faith, and it is well that we understand what it implies. It is a leading term in the vocabulary of religion.

The word grace is given prominence by Paul in his epistles. In fact we find it used in his writings twice as much as in the rest of the New Testament. Grace is the first word of greeting and the last word of farewell in his letters. For example, in II Corinthians he opens his letter by identifying himself, and then in the second verse we find these words: "Grace to you and peace from God our Father and the Lord Jesus Christ" Then he closes this letter with what is known as the apostolic benediction: "The grace of the Lord Jesus Christ and the love of God and the fellowship of the Holy Spirit be with you all" (13:14).

Paul's Christian experience was rooted in the "grace of the Lord Jesus Christ" which had sought him, found him, and forgiven him on the Damascus road. And it was this grace of Jesus Christ that now sustained him in all that he did. This grace was the secret of his penitence, humility, gratitude, and love. It freed him from resentment, ill-will, hatred, selfishness, and all that served as a barrier between himself and others. It freed him from all that made him falter on the road of service. It gave him power to overcome. It gave him strength to endure. It propelled him forward as a faithful disciple. This is why he used this word in opening and closing his letters to his friends in the faith. He was commending to them what had meant so much to him—the grace of God! Let us look at it.

What do we mean by grace? For Paul it meant the sum of all blessing that comes from God through Christ. It is the unmerited, undeserved mercy and favor that come to us from God through Christ. It is God's unconstrained love toward sinners revealed and operative in Christ. It means favor and loving kindness. We might say then that the central meaning of grace in the New Testament is God's undeserved mercy in redeeming mankind.

In Christian usage the word grace has come to mean the unmerited loving kindness of God. But it has grown to mean also the power that God imparts, to all who will let him, to overcome the impediments to victorious living. Grace then, as we understand it, is the undeserved loving kindness and power that God imparts.

It was the grace of Christ that made real to Paul the love of God which "was so vivid and compelling that perplexities could not bring despair, frustration could not limit, persecution could not make him feel an outcast, depression could not break his spirit (II Cor. 4:8-9). It was a love which altered his whole relationship to God and brought him into the liberty of a child of God. It was a bond that nothing could break, neither death nor life, . . . nor things present, nor things to come, . . . nor height, nor depth, nor anything else in all creation.' (Rom. 8:38-39). The man who knows that he is loved by God can never be defeated by life."[1]

This grace of the Lord Jesus Christ, wherein Paul's experience was rooted, became the central fact of his life, and that is why he opened and closed his letters commending his readers to the grace of God in Christ.

How do we receive this grace of God? For one thing, we must acknowledge it. When it comes to us, we must receive it. This is to know that God's grace concerns us all. It is about us all, is no respecter of persons, boundless in its abundance.

To acknowledge grace is also to expect it, to be on the lookout for God's grace, and to receive it. God's grace is offered freely to us; we do not deserve his offer. It is unmerited on our part, but comes from the loving heart of God to all his children.

To acknowledge grace is to believe that God never gives to us a task in life without giving or offering us the grace required to do it. If by chance we refuse a task which we feel has been given to us by God, then the grace that comes with the task is withheld. Refusing the task, we refuse the grace that goes with it.

To acknowledge the grace of God in Christ is to say that we believe it is always available for us and that no situation is hopeless when God's love and mercy

[1] James Reid, "The Second Epistle to the Corinthians," *The Interpreter's Bible* (Nashville: Abingdon Press, 1953), X, 424-25.

is about us. It is to say that we need never despair when we know that the grace of our Lord Jesus Christ hovers over us. It is for us to accept it.

Of course, we must desire this grace. If we turn our backs upon it, even if we acknowledge its availablity and do not deeply desire to have it, then the chances are it will not be ours to have. In other words, we must hunger and thirst after righteousness if we are to be filled. We must learn to treasure the things of heaven. Our taste for the good, the pure, and the beautiful must be cultivated, if we are to receive this grace from a good, pure, and righteous God. The desires of our hearts, the ambitions of our lives—all these are involved in receiving God's grace or unmerited favor. Do we really want it? Are we willing to receive it?

When we use what we have, God offers more. W. E. Sangster reminds us of this by saying, "We must use the present proffered grace to be able to use the grace which succeeds it." He illustrates this by telling how when he sat for his first scholarship, he was worried for fear that he would run out of paper before he had finished the exam. It seems that paper had been supplied, about six pages.

Expressing his fear to a school official, he was told not to worry; if he ran out of paper, he would find at the back of the room a gentleman in academic gown who would give him all he needed. And when he took the exam, he did run out of paper and rushed to the back of the room crying out, "Paper, paper. Give me more paper!" And he was given more paper, all that he could use.

In like manner, Dr. Sangster says, God gives us all the grace we need. But we must use what we have before we can get more. We must do the duty at hand and use the grace that comes with it, then we will have more when the next duty arrives. Always there is more to be had. We must follow the light we now have, then more light will appear for the darkness of tomorrow.[2]

God's grace is abundant and boundless, but he does not give it to us all at once. We have to use it daily with the tasks at hand, and know that there will be more for tomorrow.

Thus, may "the grace of the Lord Jesus Christ and the love of God and the fellowship of the Holly Spirit be with you all."

AIDS TO WORSHIP

Hymns: "Holy Spirit, Faithful Guide"
"There's a Wideness in God's Mercy"
Scripture: Rom. 8:31-39

A Prayer

O Lord, support us all the day long of this troublous life, until the shadows lengthen, and the evening comes, and the busy world is hushed, and the fever of life is over, and our work is done. Then, in Thy great mercy, grant us a safe lodging, and a holy rest, and peace at the last; through Jesus Christ our Lord. *Amen.*[3]

---

[2] *Can I Know God* (Nashville: Abingdon Press, 1960).
[3] John Henry Newman.

Becoming a
New Creature

We often speak of a man going from bad to worse, but seldom do we speak of a man going from bad to good. Yet the heart of the gospel truth is that a man can go from bad to good, that human nature can change for the better.

It is easy for us in these days to be suspicious of men. It is sometimes hard for us to act as though we believe a man can change.

It is easy for us to get discouraged, for we see so many things in life to give us reason for discouragement. Sometimes we wonder if God doesn't get discouraged too. When we see how cruel man can be and how callous to the finer things he can become, it depresses us and gives us concern over the future.

In fact, we have changed our ideas of human nature in recent years. We have lost the shallow optimism which prevailed during the early part of the twentieth century. Many of us can remember those days when everyone thought the world was headed for utopia.

So in the face of the shallow optimism about man our world twice has been engulfed in total war in the first half of this century, and now men are fearing the future.

We thought that by education, democracy, and better living conditions our world would change. We see now that this is not the answer. We see with eyes of pessimism how evil and sinful man can be. We see a different sort of creature from what we saw in the opening years of this century. We see to what depths of cruelty man can descend as we think of Buchenwald, Lidice, Hiroshima, and Budapest.

But distrust in human nature is not new. The Bible is full of it. In the account of the creation, soon after man's beginning in the garden, we have this sentence, "And the Lord was sorry that he had made man." For so soon did he fall. And further on we read other dissatisfactions with man. "And the Lord said, 'I will destroy man whom I have created from the face of the earth (KJV).'"

Again we read where is says, "The heart [of man] is deceitful and desperately corrupt." And Jesus never failed to see what was in man.

In the mind of the ancient Jew it was conceivable that God should be almost ready to rid himself of this troublesome creature, man. Yet, despite all our sinfulness, God holds his patience, and man continues to live. In spite of all our wickedness God continues to labor with us and love us.

Is it not because man is not all bad? That he is good too? Is it not because within us all there is the possibility of good? There is potentiality.

So we come to the heart of our subject, and that is that Christianity is both pessimistic and optimistic too. Richard S. Emrich in his book *Earth Might Be Fair* puts it like this:

"It is pessimistic about, freed from illusions about,

man's possibilities apart from God—'forasmuch as without thee we are not able to please thee'; and optimistic about man's possibilities and life's meaning when he surrenders his rebellious will to God."

This, then is the crux of the matter; there is ground for pessimism about man's possibilities apart from God. Equally, there is ground for optimism about man's possibilities and life's meaning when he surrenders his rebellious will to God.

Jesus knew this, and he spent his life trying to get man and God together. He knew what was in man. But he looked always beyond the distressing exterior of a person to what he might become. He knew that "bad as we are, we have been worse; as good as we are, we can be better."

The great problem of the world today, then, actually becomes a religious problem—a theological problem, if you please.

President Franklin Roosevelt, in the last message he wrote at Warm Springs, and which was never delivered, said this:

Today science has brought all the different quarters of the globe so close together that it is impossible to isolate them one from another.

Today we are faced with the pre-eminent fact that, if civilization is to survive, we must cultivate the science of human relationships—the ability of all peoples, of all kinds, to live together and work together, in the same world, at peace.

This involves religion and man's relationship with God.

But aside from the fact that the hope of our world rests on a religious question which has to do with man and his will and his purpose and his goodness, let us bring this closer home to ourselves.

We might indeed remain pessimistic about ourselves and our possibilities apart from God. For apart from him there is absolutely nothing for us but doom and sorrow and heartache and failure and futility. Literally, we are lost. There is no hope. We drown in our own sins. Apart from God man can do nothing. Apart from God man brings destruction upon himself.

But we have hope and optimism about our possibilities and life's meaning when we surrender our rebellious will to God. Nothing is too good to believe about life and about God when man does this.

The problems of your life, your home, and your work will find some solution when you turn your rebellious will over to God. There is always a way out. It may not be a smooth road, and there may be bumps aplenty along it, but God can help you find a solution if you will only let him.

Discord in your home can be eased and solved through God's help. Crippling habits within your own life can find help. In fact, you need not despair when you turn your life and your selfish will over to God through Christ.

All of this is but another way of saying that only the Christian way of life works. Life is really like that. We are made to be Christians. More and more

I am coming to believe that men and women and nations are lost unless God's way has control over life. It is literally Christ or chaos.

We wonder what hell is like, when we have only to look around and we can see. Hell begins right here, and so does heaven. Hell begins when a man turns his back on God, for God's way is the only way that will work. Heaven starts when a human soul is captured by Christ's spirit.

Some say, "Human nature being what it is does not change." But W. E. Hocking answers by saying, "Human nature is the most plastic part of the living world, the most adaptable, the most educatable. Of all animals it is man in whom heredity counts for least, and conscious building forces for most. To anyone who asserts as a dogma 'Human nature never changes,' it is fair to reply, 'It is human nature to change itself.'"

Down through history there have been those people who have changed the direction of their lives. They have come to a moment in life and have said, "from here on out I intend to alter my ways, to change my course of living." There have been those who have redirected their efforts towards things which are fine and good.

So before we give up all hope in man's changing, before we throw our weight on the side of common sense which does not give man the benefit of the doubt, we had better remember the twice-born men like Paul who changed the course of their lives, who rerouted their futures, who turned over new leaves.

AIDS TO WORSHIP

Hymns: "I Am Thine, O Lord"
"Lord, Speak to Me"
Scripture: Romans 12

A Prayer

Almighty God, Father of our Lord Jesus Christ, maker of all things, judge of all men: We acknowledge and bewail our manifold sins and wickedness, which we from time to time most grievously have committed by thought, word, and deed, against thy divine majesty. We do earnestly repent, and are heartily sorry for these our misdoings; the remembrance of them is grievous unto us. Have mercy upon us, most merciful Father. For thy Son our Lord Jesus Christ's sake, forgive us all that is past; and grant that we may ever hereafter serve and please thee in newness of life, to the honor and glory of thy name; through Jesus Christ our Lord. *Amen.*[1]

---

[1] *The Book of Common Prayer.*

Get Up and Walk

In the fifth chapter of John, the eighth verse, Jesus said to the man who had had an infirmity for thirty-eight years, "'Rise, take up thy bed, and walk.' And immediately, the man was made whole, and took up his bed, and walked."

This scene takes place in Jerusalem at Bethesda by the sheep gate, where there is a pool. The pool was surrounded by five arches. And under these arches a great many sick people gathered, some blind, some lame, and some with withered limbs. They waited there until the waters in the pool were moved, for the supposition was that healing would come from those waters for the sick person who first entered them.

But this man who had been coming there for thirty-eight years had never been able to get into the water first, for always someone would get in ahead of him.

Jesus confronted this man and told him to "Rise . . . and walk," but this was the very thing the man could not do. However, when he looked at Christ, he found that he could do it.

Looking at Christ we find that we can do things that in our own strength and by our own will we were never able to do. This is the Gospel, that Christ can enable us to do what we could not do. This is the Gospel, his transforming power. It is vitally related to life—"Get up and walk," "Do what you ought to do," "Do it in my strength."

The scriptures abound with impressive stories of staggering promises of what God can do in your life and mine. We are to know that no one is beyond Christ's helping hand. This scene at the pool becomes for us a vivid symbol of the power of God in human life. Too many of us have lost our faith in his power.

It is so easy for us to accept our faith as merely an inheritance to be remembered and revered and to forget that it is an experience to be entered into that is vitally related to life. Wherever religion or Christianity has grown cold, and is being ignored, we find that it had been accepted as something secondhand, and not as a throbbing, moving faith vitally related to life.

Now the man at the pool had grown so accustomed to his state after thirty-eight years that he had surely lost hope. He had accepted his lot. Considered his case closed.

And it is exactly hope that people need, a hope that will "arouse them from the lethargy of a dull, crushed acceptance of what they are, as the one thing now possible, a realization that their case has not been finally closed, and that the issue for them has not been already definitely decided." [1]

Let us look at this story and what it tells us today.

In the first place, it tells us that we must really want to be healed. Christ's opening question to this man

---

[1] Arthur John Gossip, "The Book of John," *Interpreter's Bible*, VIII, 539.

was, "Do you want to be healed?" Curious question to ask one who had been here for so long. Every day he had tried to reach the pool, but always someone would push him aside. Daily for thirty-eight years—some fourteen thousand times—he had tried to make it. But always he would crawl back to the place where he had lain so long. Here Christ looked at him and asked, "Would you like to be healed?"

This may sound like a cruel question to ask a suffering man, but we know it is the first and major question: "Do you really want to be healed?"

This question is put to us. We hear his promises of abundant life, and our hearts run out to meet and claim them. Many of us have waited longer than thirty-eight years. We have thought we wanted to accept his promises, but many of us are still by the pool. This is as far as we have gotten.

Why is it so? Because what we thought we wanted and what we said we wanted, we are not so sure we really wanted. Pascal put it like this: "Men often mistake their imagination for their heart; and they believe they are converted as soon as they think of being converted."

You see, to be Christlike at a distance appeals to us and attracts us, but at a nearer view we are not so sure. To really take Christ seriously would upset some of our comforts, would change some of our plans, would alter some of our attitudes, would realign some of our values. It is so easy to drop what Christ has just put into our hands, and go on as we are.

There was something to be said for the porches at Bethzatha. In time one grew accustomed to that way of putting in the days, came at last almost to like it. It was not unpleasant to lie there in the coolness of the shadow, while hale men, poor unfortunates, were toiling and perspiring out in the heat and glare. No doubt health is a great matter; yet, on the whole, this will do well enough for me. So, we can clearly see that Christlikeness is the gallant mode of living. But to secure it we have to pay down so much we value. Selfishness is, no doubt, a disease; yet it does bring us a bigger share of things than we could get without it. And temper is a childish ailment; but it pays. To be free of our noise and disagreeableness, folk give us what we wish. Do we want to be made whole? In theory of course, yes. But in reality and at the pinch, when we might gain it, we decide that the accustomed way of things will do. This is no idle or unnecessary question that Christ puts to us; but central, all-important, radical. And everything depends upon our answer.[2]

In the second place, this story suggests to us that God can use what we have to offer. Now this poor paralytic didn't have much to offer, but Christ said, "Get up and walk." "Use what you have!" So, he got up and walked.

What truth we see here! It tells us we are to accept ourselves because God has accepted us. And in accepting ourselves we are to offer what we have and are to him. He is forever asking, "Do you want to be healed?" Then saying, "Get up and walk."

[2] *Ibid.*, p. 541.

"Get up and walk!" How are we to walk? How are we to face life?

We are to walk in freedom as men whom God has called to newness of life. We are to walk in faith and trust, assured that life is good and that at the heart of it is a kind and loving God, personally concerned in all that we do and all that happens to us.

We are to walk as those who have nothing to fear, for perfect love casts out fear, and this love is found in Christ. We are to walk without envy and jealousy, without malice and hate, but in the light of love and goodwill. We are to walk with a mission to be used of God in the making of a better world, to follow his will and his purpose in our daily life. We are to remove from our lives all that would keep us from being our best selves, and this we cannot do by ourselves but only through his power and grace. We are to cleanse the channels of our lives so that God's waiting energies and healing power might flow through. Remember, God can use what we have.

AIDS TO WORSHIP

Hymns: "Come, Thou Almighty King"
"Walk in the Light"
Scripture: John 5:1-9

A Prayer

O God, the God of all goodness and grace, who art worthy of a greater love than we can either give or understand; fill our hearts, we beseech thee, with such love toward thee as may cast out all sloth and fear, that nothing may seem too hard for us to do or suffer in obedience to thee; and grant that by thus loving, we may become daily more like unto thee, and finally obtain the crown of life which thou hast promised to those who unfeignedly love thee; through Jesus Christ our Lord. *Amen.*[3]

---

[3] *The Book of Worship.*

Days Aren't Long Enough

The other day I saw for the first time in several years a banker friend who has been retired four years. He was erect as ever and as buoyant. I asked him how life was treating him, and he responded, "I'm fine and am enjoying every minute. The days just aren't long enough."

What a wonderful way to live in retirement and how free from the great malady of our time—boredom! When a person finds his days too short, and every minute filled to the brim, he is indeed a fortunate man. To live free of regret and free of remorse makes for joyous days. To love life and to feel at home in the universe is to know true peace of mind. To face the future unafraid and to see the past in gratitude is to live with hope. To have friends who respect you and a family who loves you is to have wealth indeed.

In reflecting upon my friend's retirement and his continued involved and active life, I am reminded of an article that appeared recently in the *National Observer* entitled, "When Pressures Stop, Will Life Be Any Fun?" It states that "the trouble with present retirement policies is that unless one is very sick there is no particular reason to slow down abruptly at 65 or any other arbitrary age. Konrad Adenauer was 73 when he began his long career as chancellor of postwar West Germany. Grandma Moses, 75 when she began her long and profitable career as an artist. Pope John XXIII was 76 when he was elevated to the papacy and began the changes and reforms that are still unfolding within the Roman Catholic Church."

It counsels that one should prepare for the problems of retirement before the day comes. I guess this involves a curtain of enjoyment of the process of life, of finding meaning and significance in it.

Robert Browning believed that each day, each year, each experience does not stand alone, that it cannot be separated from what happened before and what will happen after. Yesterday determines today, and today determines tomorrow. Therefore, live well today, and joy will be yours. I like this word from the Sanskrit:

> Look to this Day!
> For it is Life, the very Life of Life.
> In its brief course lie all the
> Verities and Realities of your Existence:
>   The Bliss of Growth,
>   The Glory of Action,
>   The Splendor of Beauty,
> For Yesterday is but a Dream,
> And Tomorrow is only a Vision:
> But Today well lived makes
> Every Yesterday a Dream of Happiness,
> And every Tomorrow a Vision of Hope.
> Look well therefore to this Day!
> Such is the Salutation of the Dawn!

David Niven admits that his "life has an improbable quality about it," but he has enjoyed every minute of it. He said "I only hope my children will be as lucky and have as much fun as their father had." Correction, "has." The screen's jaunty hero says, "I have never been in jail; I have had no feuds with prominent columnists; I don't have insomnia. My digestion seems to be in order. I've had no divorces. I love my agent, my business manager, my wife, children and mother-in-law—not necessarily in that order."

Niven carries his sense of well-being and enjoyment onto any movie set where he is working.

I guess all of us want to find joy and a sense of well-being in life. Goethe left us his secret in these noble words: "Ever-increasing endeavor; ever-widening horizons; constant renewal of the springs of life."

AIDS TO WORSHIP

Hymns: "Come, Ye That Love the Lord"
"O for a Thousand Tongues to Sing"
Scripture: Psalm 1

A Prayer

O God, who through the grace of thy Holy Spirit dost pour the gift of love into the hearts of thy faithful people: grant unto us health, both of mind and body, that we may love thee with our whole strength, and with entire satisfaction may perform those things which are pleasing unto thee, through Christ our Lord. *Amen.*[1]

[1] Sarum Breviary.

Servants of a Sacred Trust

J. B. Phillips in his translation of the New Testament translates the first and second verses of I Corinthians 4 in this way: "You should look upon us as ministers of Christ, as trustees of the secrets of God. And it is a prime requisite in a trustee that he should prove worthy of his trust."

Paul is here commending to the Christians at Corinth the apostles who are servants and stewards of a sacred trust. In his commendation he is saying that all he and his friends are trying to do is to be faithful and disinterested trustees.

Paul tells us that he has been entrusted with the glorious gospel of God. It has been given to him in trust. It was along the road as he journeyed that Jesus, whom he hated, overtook him and brought to light the things hidden in darkness. A new world opened up before Paul. Instead of persecuting, he began preaching; instead of hating, he began loving; instead of apprehending, he was apprehended. He was the inheritor of the gospel that "God was in Christ reconciling the world unto himself."

As with Paul this gospel has been given to us. We in our generation have been entrusted with it. We are the lengthened shadow of what started two thousand years ago. The gospel has come down to us from

Paul through countless thousands of followers, and we are the inheritors of this faith.

It is a sobering consideration to know that we as inheritors of the faith are this generation's representatives of the faith. The Christians of this day stand in relationship to this era just as Paul stood to his. Indeed, it makes us ask ourselves what it is we have to commend.

The prime requisite in a trustee is that he prove worthy of his trust. The true mark of trustworthiness is faithfulness. Paul again and again cited his record of stewardship and faithfulness to the trust placed in him. In spite of persecutions and trials he remained true. He counted it a privilege to suffer for Christ and wrote to his critics in Corinth that he and his friends were indifferent to both the praise and the blame of men. They were accountable only to God. They did right as they saw it with quiet disregard for public opinion. All that God expected of them was faithfulness to the trust.

Now, in our time, what about us? Are we faithful to the trust committed to our care? Do we seek to proclaim by our lives the glory of the gospel of love and grace to all we meet? Do we have a vivid sense of the fact that man cut apart from God is a poor, broken, unhappy creature? Have we found in Christ that which has changed our lives and made us into trustful, radiant persons?

Jesus, as James D. Smart reminds us, sent forth his disciples commissioning them to preach the same gospel he was preaching, to proclaim forgiveness of sins, to help set men upon their feet again. And in their training the Twelve were prepared to participate in the same ministry that was his. But in order to enter into his ministry they had first to become so one-with-him that in a measure they participated in the life he had with God. *The Spirit of God that dwelt in Jesus took up its dwelling place in the disciples and created Christ afresh in them.*

The Acts of the Apostles tells us that "what makes the church truly the church of Jesus Christ is the impartation to it of the same spirit whose mighty works had been seen in Jesus ministry." Of course, the church's possession of the Spirit is only a shadow of Jesus' full participation in it, for there is so much in the human church that blocks and resists God.

Jesus said, "You are the light of the world" (Matt. 5:14). And again, "As the Father has sent me, even so I send you" (John 20:21; or Luke 10:16). Thus this great fisher of men called his disciples to take up the same occupation and "become fishers of men" (Mark 1:17); to cast nets into the sea of humanity that men and women might be caught for the life of his Kingdom.

The implication for us is that every member of the Christian church who bears the name of Christian is an inheritor of the Gospel. And with this trusteeship comes an individual responsibility to be a witness in our time, to this generation, of the saving power of God in Christ. This is the requisite not merely of those set aside as pastors of churches, but also of all who bear the name of Christ.

When Jesus gave us our marching orders sending us into all the world, he meant for us to carry his gospel and its deeper meanings into business, industry, politics, the professions; into our homes, our play, and our solitude; yes, into the arena of everyday life.

The world today calls for changed men—men who are changed into the likeness of Christ. It calls for a church that faces the plight of men today with courage and openness. It calls for a church that is not afraid to lose itself for Christ's sake in ministering to the needs of men. It calls for a church that opens its doors to men everywhere and cries out in sincerity and in earnestness, "Come to me, all who labor and are heavy laden." It calls for a church that seeks to understand the mind of modern man and to comprehend his world, and that tries to interpret the Gospel in terms that have meaning to him. It calls for a church that is willing to risk its life for Christ's sake. May God give us such a church, and make us more worthy to be trusted with its truth!

AIDS TO WORSHIP

Hymns: "O Jesus, I Have Promised"
"More Love to Thee, O Christ"
Scripture: Eph. 6:10-20

A Prayer

Teach us, good Lord, to serve thee as thou deservest;
To give and not to count the cost;

To fight and not to heed the wounds;
To toil and not to seek for rest;
To labor and not to ask for any reward,
Save that of knowing that we do thy will;
Through Jesus Christ our Lord. *Amen.*[1]

---

[1] Ignatius Loyola.

Who Touched Me?

In Luke 8:44 we find Jesus asking, "Who touched me?" He was in the midst of a crowd of surging people, and a woman, sick and trembling, reached out her hand to touch the hem of his garment. He was sensitive to her touch and asked "who touched me?" even though the woman had darted back into the crowd.

This incident carries with it the idea of the ancient world that there is healing in a person's touch. Mothers would carry their babies miles and miles so that a holy man might touch them. Blind men would stand along the roadside just to touch the robe of a holy man.

Whether or not we feel that it is mixing superstition with faith to believe in the power of a touch, yet we do believe that a good man casts a healing influence around him. And all of us have been helped or hurt or healed by a touch. All of us believe that in a real sense we cast shadows of influence for good or ill. "Who touched me?" This question of Jesus we might well ask again today.

Wallace Hamilton in *Serendipity* reminds us that this is a question that reaches far. Many influences have touched our lives, more than we can trace. Some are so remote and obscure that we will never unravel them. Dr. Hamilton writes:

"Every person is an omnibus in which all his ancestors are riding." . . . Each of us inherited something from our parents. They touched us. But each of our parents had two parents: that's four; and they each had two; that's eight. Go back to the tenth generation, and each of us had a thousand and twenty-four parent-people; and in the twentieth generation—hold your breath now—one million, forty-eight thousand, five hundred and seventy-six! Who touched me? They touched me, a million far-off ancestors touched me. And they were not all saints back there. Those men and women out of yesterday are silently living in the house we walk around in now.[1]

Thus, heredity binds us to the past and fashions us for the future. We are a mixture. Hamilton continues: "It is something in the blood, in the bone, in the mind. No one can tell what may show up. A child may skip two generations and come up with a re-assortment of great-grandfather and Aunt Matilda. Heredity is red hair in a great-grandchild. It's a mole on the cheek. It's a way of laughing or walking or talking. It may be an unexpected spark of genius out of yesterday, or an ear for music, or an eye for beauty, or some realignment out of the remote past that we can't trace anywhere." [2]

All that past is in me. The people who have lived before me, in what they said, in the institutions they built, in the inventions they created. The past lives in us not only through this heredity strain but also through the molding influence of early childhood. Here we have all been touched.

[1] J. Wallace Hamilton, *Serendipity* (Westwood, N.J.: Fleming H. Revell, 1965), p. 88.
[2] *Ibid.*

WHO TOUCHED ME?

But it is not only our parents, and their parents, and their parents that have touched us. It is not only the influences of early childhood that have helped to mold us. We have been touched and influenced also by people we have known in our mature years who have helped to alter the course of our lives. How indebted we all are for these who have become for us what Roy Burkhart calls "radar stars." This is a term coined by Edwin Hubble, the great astronomer, who stated that in all his explorations of the heavens the most startling discovery was that of the "radar star." Some of these stars have no mass but reflect a compelling radiation power.

So, we have known people in whose presence we have come alive. They have made us dissatisfied with ourselves and determined to be bigger and better than we are. They have given us transfusions of courage, honor, insight, and dedication. How indebted we are to these persons!

Inspiration, it has been said, is largely a matter of keeping company with the inspired. These "inspired" have made a difference in my life and in yours. We cannot be the same because of them. This line of splendor got its greatest start from one man who came to live among men—a man whose coming changed the course of human history. He came as a representative of God, as God's Son, and taught that God is concerned in what happens to men, that He has a personal interest in them. He came saying, "You are important!" And when men realized what he was saying, and more that it was true, as made known in the Cross, then they stood erect as never before. They began to walk the earth as men of importance, as children of God.

The impact of his life and death and resurrection grew and was passed on from man to man, from person to person, from group to group. Today most of what we prize came from the impact of this One life, this unique, lonely Galilean, who was and is the world's greatest "radar star." It was this love that was in him, passed on from person to person in such power that it overcame the tyranny of Rome, and alone can bring peace to our world today.

As I look back over my life, I see those here and there who have been for me "radar stars." They have touched my life, and I have not been the same since. I have walked in their light. But how can you make out such a list, for as I try there are countless faces that loom up before me, whose impact have made lasting impressions on my life. Indeed, many have touched me! And many have touched you!

Frequently, the touch of another comes to us unintentionally. The person who touches us may be unaware of such an influence. Jim Ellenwood, one of the great leaders of the YMCA, said that one cold night in winter he saw his father come out from his cold bedroom to the living room and kneel down by a chair to say his prayers. Jim Ellenwood said that he was more convinced by this one simple, natural gesture of faith than by all the sermons he had heard on prayer, and his father was unaware that he was touching anyone.

Little do we realize the tremendous influence we exert when we are not conscious of it. Phillips Brooks well said, "No man or woman of the humblest sort can really be strong, gentle, pure, and good without the world being better for it, without some one being helped and comforted by the very existence of that goodness."

One loving word sets a spirit on fire, one firm handclasp renews confidence in life, and one kind deed reestablishes faith in mankind.

AIDS TO WORSHIP

Hymns: "Holy, Holy, Holy! Lord God Almighty"
"All Hail the Power of Jesus' Name"
Scripture: John 15:8-17

A Prayer

Most merciful God, who so loved the world as to give thine only begotten Son, that whosoever believeth in him should not perish, but have everlasting life: Grant unto us, we humbly pray thee, the precious gift of faith, that we may know that the Son of God is come, and may have power to overcome the world and gain a blessed immortality; through Jesus Christ our Lord. *Amen.*[3]

---

[3] *The Book of Worship.*

More Than We Are

(World Day of Prayer)

Margueritte Harmon Bro has written this arrresting line: "Of course we long to be more than we are because we are more than we are." Then, she asks this question, "Why is it that no matter how much outward success we have there is still a restless, gnawing, unrelenting desire to become more than we are?"[1]

This in a real sense is what we all want—to become more than we are. Little boys want to become great baseball players. Little girls want to finish high school when they are in the third grade, and then grow up to pick out their own clothes—to finish college, to become a doctor, or to marry and have children. Then when a girl becomes a doctor, she will still long to be more than she is.

A father will long to improve his golf scores, to increase his bank balance, to improve civic righteousness, to have peace of mind. It is as Mrs. Bro says, "Bassinet to crematory, that's us humans wishing and willing for perfection." When we reach our goals, we still are not satisfied and move those goals forward. This longing to be bigger and better than we are is with us and expresses itself in many ways, even when we settle into ruts, of irritation, illness, overeating,

[1] Margueritte Harmon Bro, *More Than We Are* (New york: Harpers, 1939), pp. 2, 3.

ceaseless activity, and an unsatisfied desire to create and achieve.

Why all this drive? Why this looking ahead for new worlds to conquer? Is it not that we want to be full-grown, complete? Is it not that we know we are meant to be bigger and better than we are? "All through our life, but especially in our youth, we have inward hints that we are children of God, containers of his nature.... We feel stymied because we have a power we are not releasing." [2]

Phillips Brooks expressed the same idea in these memorable words:

Sad will be the day for every man when he becomes absolutely content—
> With the life he is living
> With the thoughts he is thinking
> With the deeds he is doing.

When there is not forever beating at the doors of his soul, some great desire to do something larger which he knows he was meant to do, because he is still in spite of all a child of God.

Thus, man is always striving—to seek, to find, to achieve, to build, to fashion. It is man's nature to grow and to hope.

So, we long to be more than we are because we are more than we are. The real "us" is crusted over, longing to be free. We go our way trying to get at this real us within, trying to get at the power within, trying

[2] *Ibid.*

to find the key that would release it in creative living. When we cease to be disquieted, when we no longer feel the restlessness of new goals that lure us forward, then we cease to be human. Man loses his soul when he feels no pang of great desire or no pain of lofty discontent. When he loses hope, then life begins to cave in around him.

Here is a sculptor who was receiving great praise for what he deemed his masterpiece, and then on the day of his triumph he was found weeping. Asked what brought this sorrow, he said, "But you see, I am satisfied. I feel no torment of difference between what I have done and what I wanted to do. Therefore, I know that my powers have begun to decay."

So, something calls us forward, makes us restless, gives us a nameless longing. "Real peace is always mingled with the pain of longing. . . . It is a strange paradox that those who achieve the finest satisfaction know the most passionate hungers," Roy Burkhart says.

He continues, "We can only understand man if we realize that he is a bundle of desires; his soul is characterized by its outreachings. This pursuit is so basic to life that sensitive people do not know which is the greater gift—finding truth or the privilege of searching for it."

We are more than we are because God is within us and has destined us for something more. We are not just ourselves now, but we are related to him. He is our Father and we are sons and daughters of his. It is

God who lures us forward, who has placed this restlessness within. And, too, who has given us hope, which keeps us going, striving, reaching upward.

If we are to reach toward fulfillment in our inner dreams and longings, if we are to have the power within released—we must acknowledge that God holds the key. It is by him that this power is released. It is to him then that life must be oriented, and it is to him we must turn.

We reach him through Jesus Christ his Son, who becomes for us "the God for persons." Here is where he touches our lives with understanding. Here is where the great ocean of God's power touches our little shores.

There are two basic laws which are essential to our quest for released power. The first is that we must love God with our whole being—body, mind and soul. And the next law is that we must love the other person as if he were ourself. Of the two, the first is more important, for if we love God with our whole being, then it follows that we will love our neighbor. The first is hardest and more exacting.

To love God is to respect him as creator and sustainer of life. It is to reverence him in gratitude and with devotion. Francis of Assisi decided that the two great commandments were really the only directive for his life, and he set about loving God and his fellows with such joy and devotion that other young men joined him to establish the Order of the Barefoot Friars. Such power was released from within him that he became the most moving preacher of his day; when it was noised about that he was to preach, whole communities came out to hear him. Even today many look upon him as the most lovable saint of Christendom.

But, as Mrs. Bro points out,

there is always the danger that the power released through prayer may make one indifferent to what other people think and hold beyond expectation. There is also the danger that one may become exceedingly joyous, happy beyond anything previously known. . . .

One is quite right in holding back unless he is willing to run the risk of being changed. . . No doubt we would do well to pause and ponder whether we actually care to run the risk of being magnified beyond our present size, whether we want to take a chance on growing to full stature.[3]

Nevertheless, this is our approach—reflection, communion, meditation, conversation, dedication, adoration. These are words describing prayer. Just as an employer must have staff meetings and planning sessions and sales conferences, so must God have moments with us to release this power within. He must give us his orders for the day, his plans for our lives, his will for our destiny.

It is in these moments of quietness that from him flows courage and strength into our lives. Not only are his purposes made known, but also his power is given to us to see us through.

[3] *Ibid.,* pp. 11, 12.

Brother Lawrence, the humble sixteenth-century monk whose letters on the practice of the presence of God still bring strength and sustenance to countless thousands today, tells us that he was converted in this way. He meant, of course, that his life changed its direction, that he was turned about. It happened when he saw the sight of a leafless tree in winter. The thought occurred to him that if God could bless that dry stark tree to bring forth leaves, blooms, and fruit, then surely he could work a miracle in his own life. So, he started on a quest with this thought in mind—God could work a miracle in his heart. And, so he can work a miracle in your heart and my heart if we will but let him.

When we live long enough in his presence, we will discover that we are more than we are, that we belong to him, and that our destinies lie in his hands.

AIDS TO WORSHIP

Hymns: "Come, Thou Fount of Every Blessing"
"Where Cross the Crowded Ways of Life"
Scripture: Luke 2:1-13

A Prayer

Our Father, who hast set a restlessness in our hearts, and made us all seekers after that which we can never fully find; forbid us to be satisfied with what we make of life. Draw us from base content, and set our eyes on far-off goals. Keep us at tasks too hard for us, that we may be driven to thee for strength. Deliver us from fretfulness and self-pity; make us sure of the goal we cannot see, and of the hidden good in the world. Open our eyes to simple beauty all around us, and our hearts to the loveliness men hide from us because we do not try enough to understand them. Save us from ourselves, and show us a vision of a world made new. May thy spirit of peace and illumination so enlighten our minds that all life shall glow with new meaning and new purpose; through Jesus Christ our Lord. *Amen.*[4]

---

[4] *Forward Day by Day.* This was Eleanor Roosevelt's favorite prayer.

A New Commandment
(Lent)

Lent is a time of preparation for Easter, a time to contemplate the meaning of suffering and death, the cost of discipleship, and the price paid to redeem the world. It is a time to reexamine our own faulty selves against the background of that one perfect life; a time for penance, when we ask God's forgiveness for our failures; a time to discipline ourselves to do his will and to receive his love that we ourselves may more fully love.

During this season we turn our thoughts to the upper room where Jesus met his disciples just before his arrest and crucifixion. Here the Lord's Supper began. Here Jesus gave his last will and testament to his followers. He talked with urgency as if he wanted to leave his words indelibly etched on their minds: "Little children, yet a little while I am with you. You will seek me; and as I said to the Jews so now I say to you, 'Where I am going you cannot come'" (John 13:33). What does he bequeath to his disciples in these last moments? What authority does he give them that all men may know what their continuing ministry is to be? He said: "A new commandment I give to you, that you love one another."

Leonard Griffith said about this commandment: "As Christians we are not invited to love one another; we are commanded to love one another; and only as we observe this law do we retain any valid link with the historic revelation of God's love in Jesus Christ. It is this quality of love in our hearts that authenticates our Christianity before the world, declares its genuineness, and sets us apart from people who have never heard of Christ or . . . have rejected Him. 'By this all men will know that you are my disciples, if you have love for one another.' " [1]

In one sense, what Jesus was saying was not new, for others had taught this same truth. But men had never known anything like this love before. Paul described it when he prayed that his readers might "have power to comprehend with all the saints what is the breadth and length and height and depth, and to know the love of Christ which surpasses knowledge."

No word today deserves more attention than this word *love*. Basic in every marriage bond, essential to all lasting friendships, necessary in all relationships, love holds the key to that brave new world toward which we strive. Because of this Paul said, "Now abideth faith, hope, love, these three; but the greatest of these is love."

Dr. Griffith says,

The great Christians of the ages . . . are the men and women whose hearts overflowed with love. Love for every creature . . . sent Francis of Assisi on a spiritual pilgrimage that swept through a corrupt church with the purifying breadth of holiness. Love for the down-trodden and op-

[1] *The Eternal Legacy from an Upper Room* (New York: Harper & Row, 1963), p. 48.

pressed sent Lord Shaftesbury on a crusade to repeal the brutal legislation that compelled little children to toil underground in the mines for thirteen hours a day. Ecclesiastical transients who flit like butterflies from one congregation to another can be heard to ask, "Is this a preaching church? Is it a singing church? Is it a generous church?" But from the very first there has been only one question that determines the vitality and Christ-like character of a fellowship of believers: "Is it a loving church, a community of caring Christians where people . . . live, . . . worship and serve together in understanding, . . . friendship and mutual concern?"[2]

You say it is impossible to love like this. This impossibility is changed through the One who said, "Even as I have loved you, . . . love one another." Christ not only commands us to love, but offers to share with us his life; and believing that Christ is the Son of God who has conquered death and lives eternally, we also have confidence that through our faith his love can be reproduced in our lives.

A sermon of Henry Drummond suggests that if you put a piece of iron in the presence of an electrified body, the iron for a time becomes electrified. The iron is changed into a temporary magnet, and the electrified body, as long as the two stay together, shares its characteristics. So, if we put a human life in the presence of Christ, it will take on the likeness of Christ and reproduce characteristics like his.

To love, one has first to be loved. An English priest

[2] *Ibid.*, p. 52.

used to pray, "O God, help me to let thee love me." Only as we are loved can we really love. When we accept God's love in Christ, depend upon it, and receive it into every area of life, then it is we can love those around us. "This is my commandment, that ye love one another as I have loved you."

AIDS TO WORSHIP

Hymns: "Come, Thou Almighty King"
"O Love That Wilt Not Let Me Go"
Scripture: I John 3:1-11

A Prayer

Our heavenly Father, who by thy love hast made us, and through thy love hast kept us, and in thy love wouldst make us perfect: We humbly confess that we have not loved thee with all our heart and soul and mind and strength, and that we have not loved one another as Christ hath loved us. Thy life is within our souls, but our selfishness hath hindered thee. We have not lived by faith. We have resisted thy Spirit. We have neglected thine inspirations.

Forgive what we have been; help us to amend what we are; and in thy Spirit direct what we shall be, that thou mayest come into the full glory of thy creation, in us and in all men; through Jesus Christ our Lord. *Amen.*[3]

---

[8] John Hunter.

Taking It upon Himself

(Palm Sunday)

In 1935 two thousand people gathered together in the courtyard of Hull House to pay their last respects to Jane Addams, its founder. On that occasion a minister said, "If you would see her monument look around you at these thousands of people brought together in common sorrow." Why were men so moved that day? Why did tears flow so freely? It was because men realized that here was one who had given up an inherited fortune and the ease and comfort such would bring to minister to the needs of Chicago's forgotten thousands—Mexicans, Jews, Greeks. Yes, Jane Addams took it upon herself to do this not because she had to, but because she wanted; she was impelled by something within.

Today we turn our thoughts to the supreme act of all history, whose influence has lighted the world—Jesus the Christ, taking it upon himself to give his life upon a cruel cross so that mankind might see and understand the depth and height of God's love. It is here that we find the clue to God's love.

For the springboard of our thought today let us go back to that scene of Jesus hanging on the cross between two criminals when, according to Luke, one of the criminals said, "'Are you not the Christ? Save yourself and us as well.' But the other checked him, saying, 'Have you no fear even of God? You are suffering the same punishment as he. And we suffer justly; we are getting what we deserve for our deeds. But he has done no harm'" (Luke 23:39-41 Moffatt).

Here we see Jesus willing to suffer unjustly so that men might see and understand what he had been talking about. Literally, he took it upon himself. He was doing what no one could command. He was moving in the realm of "unenforceable obligations." His sacrificial act began its redemptive work immediately as one of the criminals knew that only one possessed of God would do so great a thing. Immediately his act softened a hardened life and turned it Godward. To be sure, the other thief did not understand—he did not repent—but one did.

You can't get away from love like the love of Jesus. It has a drawing power. It speaks in words all men can understand. The cross is a symbol understandable to all men, for it represents love and sacrifice beyond what is expected. It represents suffering, something known and experienced by all men. One can look at the cross and know that what Jesus was talking about he really believed.

To see something of the central place the cross holds in our faith one has but to measure the relative space given it in the New Testament, not only in the epistles but in all four gospels. And for mankind it represents above all else God's love, God's willingness to let his only Son, Jesus the Christ, suffer death upon a wooden cross that you and I might see and know through that sacrificial act the intense love of God for us. We cannot escape the drawing power of such love. It gets hold of us. So as we think of Christ taking it upon himself let us see what this cross really represents.

In the first place, the cross confronts us with the seriousness of sin: we see in it life at its worst confronting life at its best. Here is sin in all its stark reality. The fact of the cross is the result of the fact of sin. Nothing but evil in the hearts of men could have done this to a man who had done no harm.

He was one who went about doing good—healing the blind, causing the lame to walk, bringing new hope to the fallen, restoring self-respect in the outcast, pointing men to the only way of life that will work. He was kind, tender, courageous, loving. He asked of men no favors in return for the good he did except that they should give their lives to God. But cruel and evil men feared the light he brought lest it reveal the darkness of their lives and affairs. His goodness threatened their meanness, so they crucified him.

And wherever we find sin today, we can find a cross, and be reminded of that cross on Calvary's hill on which God's Son was crucified. When we are tempted to take lightly sin and to try to ignore it by calling it by other names, such as ignorance, unfulfilled good, human error or mistake, let us turn our eyes to that cross yonder outside Jerusalem and know that sin is always destructive to life. Yes, in the cross we see life at its worst confronting life at its best.

In the second place, we see in the cross the power of Christ's sacrificial act, the power of sacrificial love. "We are getting what we deserve for our deeds, but he had done no harm." The thief could not get away from that. It was too much for him, the suffering of the just for the unjust, Christ taking it upon himself. Yes, it is the supreme act of all history, and we can never escape its power. The love it demonstrates cannot be brushed aside.

A young soldier going home to Texas found his way to a tiny cottage in which a young widow and her little son Corky lived. The soldier wanted a picture of her husband, Chaplain Clark Poling, who had given his life belt to the soldier when the S.S. *Dorchester* was sinking in the North Atlantic. The soldier wanted to have a picture of the man who had given up his life for him. He could not get away from a sacrificial act like that.

This power of sacrificial love is the greatest power in the world: it melts hard hearts; it captures seasoned criminals; it causes a Judas to realize what he has done and to fling himself upon a jagged rock; it turns enemies into friends. It focuses the eyes of the world on the tiny island of Molokai when Father Damien voluntarily becomes a missionary to the lepers knowing full well he would become one too. Such a sacrificial act not only wins the concern of the world for the needs of lepers, but captivates the hearts of those lepers. It is such love which sent to Africa, David Livingstone to endure thirty attacks of a fever which would finally cost him his life, and to make more progress toward opening up the dark continent in ten years than had been made in the previous ten centuries. We cannot escape the attraction of love like that which prompted Christ to go to the cross.

God knew that the only sure way to win the hearts of men was to sacrifice his Son; and his love for all of us was so great that he was willing to do it. Men may evade and sidestep such affection for a time but can never get completely away from it.

Listen to the effect of God's love on George Tyrrell who wrote: "Again and again I have been tempted to give up the struggle, but always the figure of that strange man hanging on the cross sends me back to my task again."

AIDS TO WORSHIP

Hymns: "Crown Him with Many Crowns"
"In the Cross of Christ I Glory"
Scripture: Isa. 53:4-10

A Prayer

Lord of the great sacrifice, restrain our eagerness for the things that are seen. Thy cross is our rebuke. Increase our spending for the things eternal. Thy cross is our inspiration. Lord of the sinless life, our hope is to become like Thee. Fulfill our hearts in service, that our hope be not in vain. Lord of the holiest joy—teach us Thy grace of losing, that our joy may indeed be full. The world counteth all things lost if it gain not the things it may reckon. Help us to count all things but loss to win Thee, the wealth unmeasured. *Amen.*[1]

---

[1] Bishop Birney.

He Bore the Cross of Christ

(Good Friday)

Several years ago I had the privilege one Friday afternoon at three o'clock of joining a company of pilgrims (including priests in their brown and black robes) as they assembled in the courtyard of Pilate's praetorium in Jerusalem. A special service of worship would lead the hundreds of us down the Via Dolorosa. We would follow the traditional way of the cross from the Praetorium to Golgotha. At each of the fourteen stations of the cross we would pause for a brief reminder of what took place there and, following a prayer, would move on to the next station.

At the third station we were reminded that it was here Jesus fell for the first time with a cross; and at the fourth station, that here he met his grieving mother. Then we saw chiseled out of the wall along the street, the crude figures designating the fifth station and the words *Simone—Cyrenae*. And it is at this point that our thought for today begins.

In the fifteen chapter of Mark, the twenty-first verse, we have these words: "And they compel one Simon a Cyrenian, who passed by, coming out of the country, the father of Alexander and Rufus, to bear his Cross" (KJV).

Simon has become for Christians of all centuries a symbol of the great company of those who have been

HE BORE THE CROSS OF CHRIST

forced to carry a cross. This man ran unexpectedly into a situation which forced him to carry the cross. He was not asked to carry it; he was made to carry it. He was drafted into service and, by a power he could not resist, into being a cross-bearer. He was made to carry the cross not out of compassion for Jesus, but because Jesus was too weak to carry it (he had already fallen once). The record suggests to us that just anybody would do for the task. The soldiers chose whoever was standing by—Simon, a stranger who would not be in a position to raise objections or to cause trouble.

Halford E. Luccock in *The Interpreter's Bible* tells us that "he was probably a visitor in Jerusalem, possibly a Passover pilgrim from Cyrene in North Africa, one of the dispersed of Israel, the Diaspora. He was a passer-by, and had no connection with the tragedy that was going on. Then suddenly he was drafted into the hard role of a cross-bearer." [1]

Let us look at this story.

In the first place, it suggests to us that there are countless millions who have been forced to get under some burden not of their own choosing nor making.

Suddenly, unexpectedly, many have been singled out to bear a burden along some Via Dolorosa in life. Little white crosses mark where hundreds of thousands lie buried over the world, the army of conscripts drafted to take up the "cross" of war. Caught in wars not of their own making, they were yet forced to bear the burden of them.

[1] "The Book of Mark," VII, 901.

Again we see the host of the oppressed, the downtrodden, the hated, the despised, the slaves forced to carry the burdens of those who held power over them. Their suffering comes from the collective sins of those who set themselves against the brotherhood of man and the fatherhood of God as taught by Jesus. These burden-bearers enter into the sufferings of our Lord.

And today, we too are caught in the collective sins of past generations in man's stride toward freedom, and like Simon we cannot evade being pressed into service. As passersby we are asked in many ways to help bear the cross of liberation, and with it sacrifice and misunderstanding and some of us, loss of job and place.

Life has a way of thrusting upon us crosses of illness, which become burdens almost too heavy to bear. Suddenly and for no apparent reason we are conscripted to carry the burden of pain and suffering. "Why me?" we cry, "Why me?" We cannot fully know, but faith answers, "Why not, why not?" We do not and cannot know what life has in store for us, but we can know, as Paul said, "that in everything God works for good with those who love him."

This tells the cross-bearing sufferer, as Georgia Harkness put it, of

the abundant and unfailing resources of God for mastering pain—a sense of Divine concern, confidence that in the midst of it all there is a good to be found which, with the help of God, can lead to richer and deeper living. . . . There is no assurance that to love God will ever pay dividends in freedom from pain; there is every assurance in the Christian gospel that God will find a way to work for good in the worst situations with those who love Him and stay their lives upon Him.[2]

So, Paul Scherer suggests, Simon is a reminder to us that "a man may become involved quite unintentionally in the central drama of all the ages. Circumstances lay hold on him, and he begins as perhaps never before to understand what that lonely march to Golgotha really meant. The relentless pressure of a burden not its own shifts like the ballast of a ship in a storm to a heart that has to carry on in silence. Not just the due of pain, but pain in another's stead; not just suffering; but suffering for another's hurt; not just the routine of every day's toil, or the grim frustrations of human experience, but the weight of them taken from other shoulders, lifted from other lives. So bound up are we in the one vast bundle of life."[3]

In the second place let this story of Simon of Cyrene be a reminder not only of crosses which are involuntarily borne, but of those other crosses which are deliberately chosen. To be caught up from being a passerby into being a voluntary sharer of the cross of Christ is to be part of one of life's most important

[2] *The Gospel and Our World* (Nashville: Abingdon Press, 1949), p. 66.
[3] "The Book of Luke," *The Interpreter's Bible,* VIII, 404.

dramas. This evolution from observer to volunteer cross-bearer is the story of the Christian church. This willingness to help share the loads of others, to choose to take upon ourselves the burdens of others, to be willing to be spent in the service of Christ—this is to graduate from the elementary role of an involuntary burden-bearer to a voluntary carrier of the cross.

Much of the glory of life comes within the realm of unenforceable obligation. The story is told of George W. Rogers, the chief wireless operator at Morro Castle when it burned. "With the conflagration all around him, the floor so hot he could not keep his feet on it, the flames so close he breathed through a wet towel, when the last limit of legal or customary or enforceable obligation had long overpassed he was urged to escape, but his answer was 'I intend to stand by my post.'" In this moment, he did what no one could command him to do.

It is when we deliberately choose to bear a cross that we come into the high fellowship of Christ's suffering and discover that the cross we may be bearing becomes His cross. It is in the power of His cross that we are able to bear our cross.

AIDS TO WORSHIP

Hymns: "Above the Hills of Time"
"Jesus, Keep Me Near the Cross"
Scripture: Mark 15:16-41, 21-39

A Prayer

O Lord Jesus Christ, who as on this day didst suffer death upon the cross for us, forgive us all our sins, cleanse and make us pure. O Thou, who didst die that we might live, let us not grieve Thee by our sins, but soften our hard hearts, and bend our wills, that we may hear Thy voice and live. O Thou, who for us didst bear bitter sufferings, and dost not send us more than we are able to bear, give us help and strength to bear meekly and patiently all our troubles, and to forgive as we hope to be forgiven. Give us grace and strength so to live in this world, that at last we may dwell in that home which Thou by Thy death didst win for us; for Thine own Name's sake. *Amen.*[4]

---

[4] H. W. Turner.

The Future Belongs to Love

(Easter)

The future belongs to love. It belongs to love because love is a language everyone can understand, and that everyone can speak if he will. "A loving, kindly glance, or word, or shake of the hand, a simple deed, is recognized in every land." This is why Henry Drummond called his little book about love *The Greatest Thing in the World*.

The future belongs to love because love enriches him who gives it as well as him who receives it.

But even more, the future belongs to love because it belongs to God, and God is love. All hatred, falsehood, fear, cruelty, enmity, and bitterness are doomed by love.

The resurrection of Christ is the symbol telling us that victory belongs to love, that evil and hatred cannot hold sway over it.

When we see the cross, let us be reminded that the future belongs to love and let us make love our aim. We cannot escape love for in the end it will win. God so loved the world that he gave his Son because of divine love. The cross confronts us with the heights of love. From the despair of sin we move to the hope of divine love. The cross lifts into clear relief God's unconquerable love for us. All understanding of the cross must start with the love of God.

The cross and its attendant sufferings were the only course open for God, through which his children as free moral agents could understand his love and desires for them. "If it be possible, let this cup pass from me." In other words, if there be any other way . . . but there wasn't.

Now that we have the cross we know as never before what love really means. Here is Jesus exhibiting the loving heart of God, suffering because of sin, and longing with intensity for men to be reconciled, and to return to the Father.

Love is not only a language everyone understands, but love is a contribution everyone can make. The meekest and the humblest can have a part. The contribution you and I make in life will not go unfelt but will play its part in the ongoing drama of life. The Christian cause began with the man of Nazareth and his Galilean friends. On that bleak, first Good Friday when his cause seemed doomed on the cross, the stream of salvation rolled on, and love finally won and has been winning ever since. The stream has now become an ocean of love. How could it have prospered apart from the contribution of little people like ourselves?

Real love has a magic power. You can feel its healing influence; it has a presence all it own. You can tell when a person loves you and feels kindly towards you. Love conveys a message even without words. It assumes an attitude. It radiates a warmth.

You can feel the presence of love in a church. In some churches there is an atmosphere of real love and warmth and compassion. In others there is coldness and an aloofness; there is an unconcern, an indifference. Oftentimes the atmosphere without the church controls that within. If there is bitterness within a community, sometimes it spills over into the church.

But the church which is true to the Lord radiates love and compassion and concern. It loves the unlovely: it pays for the unworthy; it forgives the penitent sinner. It becomes a hospital for the helpless, a shelter for the wayward, a hospice for the lonely. It is a light for the darkness.

We can show our love for Christ by being loyal to his Church. We can be part of a blessed fellowship within the church and refuse to engage in church quarrels. We can uphold the church, and we can help the church to grow and to reach out and to lift up fallen humanity with love.

I wonder what energy would be sent out from our churches if every Sunday all who worshiped would push out hatred and ill will from their hearts and let love reign.

Yes, love is a contribution everyone of us can make.

AIDS TO WORSHIP

Hymns: "O For a Thousand Tongues to Sing"
"Christ the Lord Is Risen Today"
Scripture: Matthew 28

A Prayer

O Blessed Lord, we beseech Thee to pour down upon us such grace as may not only cleanse this life of ours, but beautify it a little, if it be Thy will, before we go hence and are no more seen. Grant that we may love Thee with all our heart, and soul, and mind, and strength, and our neighbour as ourself, and that we may persevere unto the end; through Jesus Christ our Lord. *Amen.*[1]

---

[1] James Skinner.

The Jobs We Do
(Labor Day)

Some time ago I saw in an advertisement in a weekly magazine these words, "The Greatest News for the Human Race in 1900 Years!" The news was this: "Science gives you longer life." The ad said that in the days of the Roman Empire the average length of life was twenty-three years. In the United States it had climbed to forty years by 1850 . . . to forty-nine by 1900. And now the average life-span here is over sixty-seven years, and life expectancy is still increasing."

In another paragraph these words were printed: "This tremendous increase in life expectancy gives us many more years to enjoy the blessings of the earth."

Whether we will enjoy the blessings of earth depends upon our finding meaning in the jobs that we do.

The tragedy of these times is that so many millions of people have lost the sense of dignity of the day's work. They see no real meaning in their jobs. A job is just something that has to be done to keep soul and body together. Apart from the weekly pay envelope or the monthly check there is no meaning in it.

Some hold the same idea of work as did one hitchhiker who said to another, "That's right, just sit there and let me work my finger to the bone."

But surely if you and I are going to find joy in life

and satisfaction in the days of our years, we must see meaning and purpose in our work.

To the Greeks work was something to be left to slaves or mechanics. Aristotle's perfect man "will not soil his hands." Therefore, the Greeks made little achievement in natural sciences as contrasted with their achievement in philosophy or mathematics.

The Hebrews regarded work as a divine command from which no man was exempted.

All through the Scriptures, work is a divine ordinance. Paul said, "If any will not work, neither let him eat" (II Thess. 3:10). Work is neither a curse nor a punishment, but an integral part of God's original intention in the creation of the world.

Our Lord glorified work. He was a village carpenter. So, work is a law of God for human life.

At the outset let us realize that every job has its own set of difficulties and its own set of satisfactions. Sometimes the job that we have seems to be made up only of unpleasant aspects. The detail and the routine almost get us down. Then we think of someone else's job, and we see in it only pleasantness. We forget that every job is made up of both aspects.

This leads us to another consideration, namely, in order that our work may have more meaning, we should try and see how our little jobs are part of a larger setting, a nobler scheme. When we see what we are doing as part of the great scheme of things, we become conscious that we are making a contribution to the common work of the world.

Of course we must recognize that some work seems to be more worthwhile than other, and that some is not worthwhile at all. Some does not serve mankind. There are jobs which good men are ashamed to enter and which others leave because they are not worthwhile.

All of us want to feel that what we are doing is worthwhile, that our efforts are being directed toward some achievement no matter how modest. We dislike coming to the end of our days and feeling that all we have done is carry bricks up a hill and then carry them down again, that we have merely gone through the motions.

Life is unbearable unless it has real meaning, and the way for it to have meaning is for us to be engaged in work which we know is contributing to some larger whole.

We need to enlarge our idea of *vocation* and see that the world is one, secular and sacred, and that the chief way to serve the Lord is in our daily work. The salvation of the world will come not merely by the efforts of missionaries and church workers, but by the efforts of all who are deeply committed.

Thus, there can be in reality one vocation but many professions. Some persons can contribute to the conversion of the world by working in banks, in hospitals, in mills, in grocery stores.

If we could but see in our work its larger meaning, then our jobs would take on new significance. The work of a bricklayer is magnified if it helps to build a cathedral; sweeping a hotel room can be important if it helps to re-create the lives of those who occupy that room so that they may devote themselves to some high goal.

We want to do work that will last. The psalmist in Psa. 90:17 speaks of this desire when he prays the words which form our text: "Establish thou the work of our hands, O Lord."

To live on this level is to "try to write a poem which will enrich the experience of persons still unborn, to build a garden wall that will grow in beauty with the years, to produce a law that will help to insure future justice."

AIDS TO WORSHIP

Hymns: "This Is My Father's World"
"Rise Up, O Men of God"
Scripture: Psa. 90:14-17

A Prayer

O Lord of souls, who hast chosen and called us to service in thy Church; all our trust is in thee, for in thee are the springs of our life. Abundantly give us of thy blessed Spirit, without whom nothing is strong, nothing is holy, and use us as it shall please thee for the glory of thy Name. Empty us of self and fill us with the meekness of wisdom. Increase our faith, mellow our judgment, stir our zeal, deepen our affections. Do thou choose for us the work we do and the place in which we do it, the success we win and the harvest we reap. Preserve us from jealousy and impatience, from self-will and depression. Make us faithful unto death, and give us at last the crown of life; through Jesus Christ our Lord. *Amen.*[1]

[1] *Prayers New and Old.*

Living in Expectation

(Advent)

In Luke 2:38 we have these words: "She gave thanks to God, and spoke about the child to all who were living in expectation of the liberation of Jerusalem."

It refers to a group of people in the Israel of Jesus' day who were living in expectation of the liberation of Jerusalem. This small group of people as James Moffatt translates it, were on the "outlook" for the Messiah who would free them from the bondage of Rome. For centuries their prophets had warned them of his coming and had told them to be on the lookout for the man who would be their Savior.

In a real sense, nothing really great has ever happened except where there was a group of "sentinel souls" living in expectation of it. Arthur J. Gossip in his book *The Galilean Accent* says that "They are the kind of folks by whom the world moves forward, who live in a qui vive of expectancy, always standing on tiptoe, always sure that something big may happen at any time."

Going back to the Old Testament we can trace this note of expectancy which culminated with the entrance of Jesus. People for years had been expecting the Messiah. His coming is even referred to in Genesis, and in Isaiah we find these words,

> For to us a child is born,
> to us a son is given;

> and the government shall be upon
> his shoulder,
> and his name will be called
> "Wonderful, Counselor, Mighty God,
> Everlasting Father, Prince of Peace."

Later on we find that "when the time was fulfilled, Jesus came." And so it happens throughout life. Great movements and revivals come when men are living in expectation of them.

Only as we live in expectation do we live at all. Living like this brings a response from within ourselves. It is facing life with a positive attitude and serves as a tonic for the soul. Living in expectation of liberation means that we expect the best from ourselves. We have confidence and faith in the possibilities that are within us. We believe that God has something definite for us to do in this world, however humble it may be, and we therefore are on the lookout for it.

One of the tragedies of our time is the number of men and women, boys and girls who have lost faith in themselves, who have lost the zest for living. But living with a positive note will help to bring out the best within a person. Many young people today are defeated before they start. They feel that they can neither rise higher than the environment into which they were born nor transcend the level of their heredity. They feel that their future and lot are completely determined by the conditions into which they were born. But man can rise above his inheritance.

LIVING IN EXPECTATION

Let us turn now to the effect this law of expectancy has on other people. People respond to what is expected of them. If you expect something good from a person, this expectation tends to bring out that good in him. If you treat a person kindly, that person will tend to respond in like manner. Loving a person arouses in him a similar response. What do you expect from people? What do you expect in them? The answers to this determines the quality of your Christian character.

A very close friend of mine tells the story of one of her teachers who expected big things from her. The teacher believed in the girl, and by believing in her made the girl believe in herself. The teacher's encouragement made her study hard and try to measure up to the confidence placed in her. She went into class a poor math pupil; she came out an A student because she responded to what was expected from her.

We have all witnessed this law at work. You recall that Will Rogers once said that he had never met a man he didn't like, that he could always find something good in people. Men responded to his faith and gave Will their friendship.

In the story of Stanley's meeting with David Livingstone in the heart of Africa, one thing in particular stands out. On the occasion when Stanley struck an ignorant native for stealing his watch, Livingstone said, "Stanley, don't do that! Men always respond to the way you act toward them." In other words, hate breeds hate, bitterness, bitterness, goodness begets goodness, and love, love.

Turning our thought around a little and going deeper, we find that God too responds to this law. God in a real sense can only touch the soul that lives in expectation, the soul that lives by faith. Only as we pray, believing, does God answer our prayers. Only as we go to him in anticipation of feeling his presence does God actually commune with us. This does not mean that he is dependent upon this law, for we know that at times he does thrust himself upon a person in the most unexpected moment, such as with Paul on the road to Damascus. Many times God has made himself known in sorrow and trouble. But what I am saying is, that we are dependent upon this law if we are to know God. Living expectantly conditions us so that God can move in. In other words, to live expectantly means to open the door to our lives, lift the latch, and invite him in.

Expecting the best in men; keeping on the outlook for God's coming; expecting that his church will bring changes in the lives of us all; living like this means that we must not only look for good but live for it. With such expectancy comes a definite commitment, a willingness to live so that what we are expecting may come. It means that we must expect good things so much that we will try and bring them about.

One only lives, as one lives in expectation. What a joy to live like this—expecting God to guide you, expecting him to be true to you, expecting the best from yourself, expecting prayer to work, expecting something to happen to you when you worship. "She gave thanks to God about the child and spoke to all who were living in expectation of the liberation of Jerusalem."

AIDS TO WORSHIP

Hymns: "Come, Thou Almighty King"
"Faith of Our Fathers"
Scripture: Isa. 40:1-5

A Prayer

O Thou who art the source of all existence and the light of all seeing: We remember with joy and awe that the world is thy creation, and that life is thy gift. Lift up our thoughts from the littleness of our own works to the greatness, the majesty, and the wonder of thine, and teach us so to behold thy glory that we may grow into thy likeness; through Jesus Christ our Lord. *Amen.*[1]

---

[1] *The Book of Worship.*

Our Bible Comes Alive

(Universal Bible Sunday)

In spite of the fact that the Bible is a best seller, to millions of people it is a closed book, and to thousands of Christians it is a seldom-opened book.

Why is the Bible so little read by so many people, especially by so many Christians? For one thing, it is because many do not read it sufficiently to appreciate its contents and its value for us today. Many feel that it seems to speak to another age and not for today. Others feel that it appears to conflict with modern-day knowledge. And then too our materialistic and secularistic age has crowded it out. Then, many do not know, or do not try to find out, the situation out of which each passage came and the purpose for which it was written.

We believe that the Bible should be an open book with wide distribution, and that there is value in reading it whether it is completely understood or not. We believe that it has a message all its own and speaks not only to the mind, but also to the heart. We believe that God speaks to men today from the pages of this book and that there is great value in the reading of the Scriptures.

Although we believe that there is value in reading the Bible even without complete interpretation or understanding, on the other hand, we also believe that to fully appreciate it a person must know as much as he can about the conditions out of which it arose, why it was written, and to whom it was directed.

What is the Bible? Of course we believe that it is the Word of God, but this Word is really a library containing sixty-six books. Each of these books is a separate unit. The oldest was written about 3,000 years ago and the most recent approximately A.D. 150. It is literature which contains history, legend, poetry, drama, and law.

This library is divided into two sections—the Old Testament and the New Testament. The Old Testament contains thirty-nine books and was written in Hebrew. The Old Testament is a history of a people, the Hebrew people. To quote another:

It tells the fascinating story of patriarchal life, the disappointing sojourn in Egypt, the weary wilderness wanderings, the rough bloody conquest of Palestine, the gradual formation of the monarchy, the tempestuous period of the Kingdom, the humiliating carrying away into Babylon, the adventurous return from exile, and the heroic and perilous days of Judaism in a land stripped of her ancient glory.

Through it all God is at the center of every aspect of life. He was at the center of Hebrew life—family, work, school, national life, political life, common life. Thus, for these people religion was interrelated in all affairs of their concern.

The New Testament is the history and literature

of the Christian movement and contains twenty-seven books, all written in Greek. About it was written

> Jesus is the central figure. An infant church is organized after his death. A matchless missionary moves back and forth over the Graeco-Roman world. Churches were established in strategic centers and letters were written by Paul to establish them in the faith and direct their growing life. Other literature came into being. In time some of the literature came to be regarded as being more sacred than the rest. The selective process went on, church councils gave their confirmation, and our New Testament in its present form became a reality.

The Bible is not only a library of sixty-six books, containing an Old Testament giving a history of the Hebrew people, and a New Testament giving the history and literature of the Christian movement, but it is also the Word of God giving the record of man's religious experience. Thus, it is a book of religion.

It is not a textbook of science or even of history, but a book of life or spiritual experience of God in the soul of man. In this book we discover man's most significant quest, his quest for God.

Here we find not only man's search for God, but God's progressive revelation to man. Thus, it is a book of revelation, for through it God revealed himself to man. It is an account of a remarkable evolution in man's idea of God. Before Moses appeared, man worshiped God at local shrines; a stone, an oak tree, a mountain would do. Then after Moses the worship of God took place at the central Ark of the Covenant. Finally the place of worship was located in Jerusalem, and Jehovah became a national deity rather than a tribal God.

Then came the prophets, who rescued man from devotion to a national deity with manlike passions and preached the moral character of God. For Amos, God was a God of justice; for Hosea a God of kindness; and for Isaiah a God of holiness. Then, Micah proclaimed him all three. So we find in the Old Testament man's growing idea of what God is like. God did not change but man's conception of him did. Or to put it another way, God progressively made himself known.

Then, of course, Jesus Christ came, and God through Christ made himself known in a form that man could understand. Christ became the bridge between heaven and earth. Paul put it like this in II Cor. 5:19; "God was in Christ reconciling the world to himself." Jesus gives us a clue to what God is like. In him we know the nature of God. Or in other words in him we find the near side of God—the God for persons.

It is here that the human and the divine meet as God reveals himself in the life of Jesus Christ. Here is the supreme revelation for us.

But it does no good for us to know that the Bible is a book of religion describing the religious experiences of a group of people, and that it is a book of revelation in which God makes himself known, unless we also discover that it can be a book of religion for us and that God through it can make himself known to us today. Paul B. Kern was hinting at this when he wrote: "The Bible upon the mythical center table of the home will never save the nation; but the Bible as the daily spiritual sustenance of the family and the individual will undergird us with a righteousness and peace and power."

Saturate yourself with the truths of this great book. Your whole life will be lifted; your faith will be more robust; your love will be warmer; your courage will take on new life, as you hear God speaking through Jesus: "And, lo, I am with you alway even unto the end"; "heaven and earth shall pass away, but my words shall not pass away"; "I am the way, and the truth, and the life"; "Come, follow me."

AIDS TO WORSHIP

Hymns: "O God, Our Help in Ages Past"
"Holy Spirit, Faithful Guide"
Scripture: Psa. 119:105-12

A Prayer

Lord, give us a heart to turn all knowledge to Thy glory, and not to our own. Keep us from being deluded with the lights of vain philosophies; keep us from the pride of human imaginations, but in all things acting under the good guidance of the Holy Spirit, may we find Thee everywhere, and live in all simplicity, humility, and singleness of heart unto the Lord. *Amen.*[1]

[1] Henry Kirke White.

Christmas Is a Time for Giving

The kind of Christmas we will have this year will depend in large measure upon the kind of gifts we include on our lists.

Certainly Christmas is a time of giving, and for many this makes it a time of dread. But let us think for a little while of some giving that we should not overlook.

In the first place Christmas is a time of giving up.

It is a time of giving up fear.

Alistair MacLean tells of one of the most dramatic scenes in European history. When Charles VIII of France demanded ransom from the free city of Florence, Capponi, the mayor, refused to give him anything. And Charles thundered threats. "I will have my trumpets blown," he cried. "Blow your trumpets," answered Capponi, "blow your trumpets, and we will ring our bells." Then Charles fell silent for he knew the ringing of the bells would bring forth the hidden army of Florence.

Charles M. Crowe says that this story symbolizes the resources of the Christian in the face of the blustering threats of life. We read "Behold, I bring you good tidings of great joy. . . . For unto you is born this day in the city of David a Saviour, which is Christ the Lord" (KJV).

Since that first announcement, the Christian has

had ringing in his heart bells of joy which drive out fear.

There is so much in life to burden us and make us sad. We have so many doubts and heartaches, so many disappointmetns and fears. But Christmas is a time when we give up our fears.

Again Christmas is a time of "giving out," real giving, not just swapping. It is a time of giving and not expecting something in return. It is a time for the outpouring of human kindness.

Whatever is given, it's genuine significance lies in the thought or motive behind it. A child's bunch of wild daisies given to his mother in love means more than an expensive orchid given with no thought of affection.

The real value of a gift is dependent upon the motive or thought behind it. Gifts which carry with them kindness and thoughtfulness are the ones that are lasting and that make a difference. It is not so much the size or cost of a gift as the heart and attitude of the one who gave it.

When we are giving out this year, let us add those gifts of affection and love that can be given without cost. "Silver and gold have I none"—but love and kindness we may have, and these money cannot buy. A word of cheer, an expression of faith, a note of appreciation—such things add joy to Christmas.

There are millions in our world today who are starving for the milk of human kindness. There are bruised spirits suffering from hastily spoken words and harsh deeds who long for the sympathy that comes from a heart filled with love.

Finally, Christmas is a time of "giving in"—of surrender to Christ, of acceptance of him as King, of receiving God's greatest gift in the heart. It is a gift that money cannot buy. It is merely to be accepted. "For God so loved the world that he gave his only Son that whoever believes in him should not perish but have everlasting life."

If we miss "giving in" to this gift, miss receiving it, then we do indeed miss Christmas. Without this gift there would be no Christmas. No wonder the angels sang, "Fear not: for, behold, I bring you good tidings of great joy, which shall be to all people. For unto you is born this day, in the city of David a Saviour, which is Christ the Lord" (KJV).

And the shepherds responded, "Let us go over to Bethlehem and see this thing which has happened." They accepted the gift of God. They gave in to him.

Since that early day men have not been able to get away from God's truth, his insight, his interpretation, his way of life. Men have ignored him for expediency's sake, but have had to return to him for their own sake.

Christmas then is a time to give in to God, to accept his offer. We see Christ look into the eyes of a Magdalene and watch her gain mastery over her possessions; we watch him dine with dishonest Zacchaeus and see Zacchaeus give up his ill-gotten gains; we watch Christ lay hands on a shiftless, faithless Simon and see Simon transformed into Peter the Rock.

Today we see Christ across the centuries as one who still gives men power to change and power to conquer.

Let's "give in" to God this Christmas and take him at his word. Let's accept God's gift as our very own.

AIDS TO WORSHIP

Hymns: "Joy to the World"
"O Little Town of Bethlehem"
Scripture: Matt. 2:1-10

A Prayer

O almighty God, who by the birth of thy holy child Jesus hast given us a great light to dawn upon our darkness: Grant, we pray thee, that in his light we may see light. Bestow upon us, we beseech thee, that most excellent Christmas gift of charity to all men, that so the likeness of thy Son may be formed in us, and that we may have the ever brightening hope of everlasting life; through Jesus Christ our Lord. *Amen.*[1]

---

[1] William Bright.